HOW TO BE MADE WHOLE

An answer to the whole question

ROBIN STEELE

WESTBOW
PRESS®
A DIVISION OF THOMAS NELSON
& ZONDERVAN

WestBow Press books may be ordered through booksellers or by contacting:

WestBow Press
A Division of Thomas Nelson & Zondervan
1663 Liberty Drive
Bloomington, IN 47403
www.westbowpress.com
1 (866) 928-1240

Content Editor: Deborah Azzolini
Line Editor: Elizabeth Wharton
Cover Artwork: Michelle Hagerty
Cover Layout: Luke Tharp

Library of Congress Control Number: 2020902308

ISBN: 978-1-9736-8525-8 (sc)
ISBN: 978-1-9736-8526-5 (hc)
ISBN: 978-1-9736-8524-1 (e)

Printed in the United State of America.

WestBow Press rev. date: 02/26/2020

WHAT PEOPLE ARE SAYING ABOUT

HOW TO BE MADE WHOLE

This book speaks to all of God's people. This positive message is about overcoming challenges that life presents you and not allowing circumstances to dictate your future. Kennady's story is an inspiration, led by the God-given love and acceptance of two wonderful people—Robin and Erica. Enjoy, be amazed, but most of all hear the love that our God has for us all.

—**Dennis Franchione**, *former head football coach at Alabama and Texas A&M Universities*

Robin shares an incredibly hopeful and inspiring message that points us all to Christ and reminds us that He knows what is best for each of us, even when things don't go as we expect them to. Robin has continuously brought us to tears and moved our hearts through his family's story. You will be amazed, inspired, and encouraged.

—**Claire Culwell**, *International speaker and author, twin abortion survivor*

In this book, Robin masterfully illustrates that what God says about us far outweighs what anyone else may think about us. The revelation that God has given Robin in this book is truly incredible. You'll begin to feel the power in it the minute you begin to read his story. Thank you, Robin, for sharing your family's story with the world. I'm better because of it!

—**Jeremy Foster**, *lead pastor of Hope City*

In this inspiring book, Robin shares how God's Word has come alive through the arrival of their firstborn daughter, Kennady. As you face difficult challenges in life, this is a resource you will reference again and again. Prepare to be greatly encouraged!

—**Joseph Sangl,** *founder of I Was Broke, Now I'm Not, CEO of INJOY Stewardship Solutions*

How to Be Made Whole tells the story we all want and need to hear—that our lives can matter regardless of what we face, or what we feel unable to achieve. Robin, Erica, and Kennady are heroes to our family. Their story is contagious and resounds with God's love and affirmation. You will be inspired and equipped to live a meaningful life.

—**John Ragsdale,** *senior pastor of The Hills Nashville*

At first glance, this is a book about Kennady Steele and her story of God's grace and meaning for her life. But as you read this book, you'll discover it's far more than just her story—it's ours as well. How do you begin to process being told your daughter may not have a meaningful life, nor be normal? What does it mean to have a purpose-filled life, and how do you embrace the challenges that come your way? Her story is our story—a journey of God's work in all of our lives. And what we learn is that a meaningful life is not about what we know, nor is it what we do – it is about WHO we are in the eyes of our Lord. May this book speak to you as you hear God whisper in your ear His love and affirmation of you.

—**Tom Thomson,** *senior vice president of World Help*

There is no greater, life changing truth than to know that God not only sees us deeply but loves us unconditionally. The hope we find in this book reminds us that the moments of our greatest pain can be redeemed and used for our good and God's glory!

—**Tauren Wells,** *Grammy nominated,*
Sony Music Recording Artist

CONTENTS

ACKNOWLEDGEMENTS

Thanks to my PromiseLand Staff and Family! You are an incredible foundation for me to find strength.

Thanks to all our blog and social media family! Your comments and posts are so encouraging to us.

Thanks to Deborah Azzolini! You provided the exact voice I needed to get my heart out on paper.

Thanks to my boys, Jude and Avery! You provided a sweet diversion when things were busy.

Thanks to my wife, Erica! You believed in me and pushed me to keep going.

Thanks to Kennady! You are the star.

Thanks to Jesus! You give the star her light.

DEDICATION

This book is dedicated to all the people longing for meaning,
Those who are waiting for something to be fixed,
Those who carry a really tough load,
And those whose voice will never be heard.

FOREWORD

Many of us believe that life is formulaic. Especially, if you are a believer in Jesus Christ. In other words, if I accept Jesus Christ into my life and live righteously according to Biblical principles, I will live a life unscathed. Untouched by tragedy. Robin and Erica Steele would fit that assumption perfectly. They grew up in my church. Full of integrity and love for God. They came from amazing parents who helped start our church, fund the church, and brought many lost souls to grow the church. Robin and Erica perfectly fit the life that we would want everyone to have. He became our student pastor, then our children's pastor and, ultimately, they became lead pastors of a thriving church in San Marcos. Perfect life. All the boxes were checked...and then.

Everybody gets an "and then." The email, the phone call, the summons to the doctor's office, the boss asks you to step into his office.

I will never forget getting a call from Robin Steele to inform me his daughter had been born. His tone was measured and mature—very unusual for such exciting news. On the other hand, I was over the moon for Robin and Erica—their first precious baby was here. I was a bit taken aback by Robin's tone in light of this amazing event so I asked the question, "Is everything ok?" In the same mature, matter-of-fact tone, Robin's answer broke my heart. Denise and I immediately drove to the hospital. Amid the tears and the hugs was the presence of the Holy Spirit. Peace that passes all understanding. If God ever entrusted a couple with a special gift, he found the right ones. We have watched how Robin and Erica have walked this road with grace given by God to encourage others who have experienced pain.

Robin Steele's *HOW TO BE MADE WHOLE* touched my heart and changed my mind. I could not put the book down. All of us are desperate for wholeness. With practical steps and storytelling that will touch your soul, you will thank yourself for reading and absorbing the testimony of Robin and Erica Steele.

I'm so proud of Robin and Erica, their flourishing church, their friendships and their impeccable character.

—**Randy Phillips,** *lead pastor of Life.Family,*
founder of PHILLIPS CRAIG & DEAN

PART ONE | What is the WHOLE Question?

CHAPTER ONE

LITTLE SAMMY

Little Sammy crawled around the blanket like an army tank heading into the front lines. He was just under a year old and full of life. However, as Sammy played on the living room floor, his parents began to notice that he did not respond to their voices. At first, they thought maybe he was too preoccupied with his toys, but, quickly, they recognized that he could not hear them. After a battery of tests and doctors' visits, they concluded that little Sammy was deaf. His parents were lost. They lived in a tiny town in the Midwest with little resources or knowledge of the deaf community. Until age five, Sammy had no language.

I recently sat down with Sam, now 62 years old. Through a sign language interpreter, he told me his life story; I was astounded at the complexity of his journey. Near the end of our conversation, I asked Sam a deep question, "Sam, is it possible to be a deaf person and a whole person at the same time?"

CHAPTER TWO

ME BEFORE HER

I remember noticing back in elementary school that I was shorter than most of the other kids. At recess, I was always the last one picked for a basketball team. Regardless of my speed or agility, my shortness spoke the loudest. As I grew older, it moved from the basketball court to my dating game. Often, I thought, *Wow, she is pretty…but she is taller than me.* We all know the unwritten rule about dating: The guy needs to be taller than the girl (or at a bare minimum, the same height). That rule worked squarely against me! For years, I struggled with my height and how it compared to other students, coworkers, competitors, and the general public. If only I were 3 inches taller, I would be able to date anyone I wanted (yeah, right!). I would be able to stand eye to eye with employers and peers. I could compete toe-to-toe on the field or court. I would not have to work extra hard to fit in. Thankfully, I lived in Texas where boots are always trending. Cowboy boots became my secret hack! I could don a pair of trusty boots with tall heels and claim those missing inches!

As if height were not enough, when I was in junior high school, I was cursed with the most embarrassing of teenage issues: acne. Oh my goodness! It was eighth grade at Dahlstrom Middle School, and I had an excessive amount of acne. I pummeled myself with negative thoughts like, *I'm short, and I have zits! What in the world? If I stand a chance with the girls, I can't have all these ugly things all over my face!* I remember standing in front of the mirror counting the pimples. One day I counted ninety-three! I would ask myself what I had done to deserve this. I felt like I was reliving one of the plagues of Pharaoh in Egypt. God gave him pimples, right?

I tried to accept my pimpled face as one of my "Egyptian plagues" and resign myself to the fact that there was nothing I could do about it, but I could not. To fix this significant problem, I tried every kind of cleaner I could find: washes, soothing creams, stinging pads, soaps. My mom and I read in a magazine that chocolate was the culprit, so I went on an immediate chocolate fast. No improvement. Finally, we went to a dermatologist who prescribed a strong medication. I started to experience relief, and I thought that acne might not destroy my life after all. I hacked my height issue and the Egyptian plague of my life!

In high school, I was a fairly decent soccer player. I promoted to the varsity team my freshman year and played well. As a result, I lettered and was able to order the coveted letter jacket. There is nothing in high school quite like the day you get your letter jacket. It could be ninety-five degrees in June, but you are going to wear that jacket all day long like there is a blizzard outside. You are sweating, but alas, you are cool. You are, after all, a letterman. What's more, most people do not letter until they are juniors or seniors, so as you can imagine, I was pretty proud of myself and my saunter showed it.

The following summer our soccer coach left our school, and we got a new coach. Ironically, our new coach did not know anything about soccer. His experience had been in basketball and football, where height played a significant role. To select the team, He lined us all up on the side of the field and selected the tallest players to play varsity. Unjustly, I landed on the junior varsity team. What an insult! I was so hurt, offended, and livid. I remember wearing my letter jacket as I loaded the bus for our first game. I was hoping he would see the jacket and suffer internal conflict about his terrible choice to demote me from my rightful spot on varsity.

I'm sure you can imagine what I did when the game began. With rebellion and anger running through my veins, I played the most inspired soccer game of my life! I was all over the field, running, kicking, passing. We were down 0-1 in the second half, and my business was unfinished. I had a point to prove and prove it I did. I scored two points late in the half, and we won the game.

By the end of the season, I was back on the varsity team, beaming with pride and reveling in vindication. When my high school soccer career finally ended, I had been selected to first team All-District.

As I grew older, the challenging scenarios continued to roll in, and I continued to face challenges head-on, set on fixing each problem through my determination and will power. I distinctly remember studying for my first exam as a freshman at Texas State University. In high school, teachers would hold our hands through the testing process. They would serve repeated reminders, prepare us for each test, provide worksheets, and emphasize important content. They would even give us second chances if we didn't do well the first time! When I arrived at college, I was stunned with the new reality that the success or failure of my education relied solely on my ability to prepare, study, think, work hard, ask questions, and own every part of the process.

I was scared as I prepared for my first college-level biology exam. It was covering about four weeks of material, and there were no worksheets or homework to review. The professor offered no hints or clues as to what the test would cover. All I had to prepare with was a colossal textbook and any notes I had taken in class. How could I possibly prep for such a daunting task? To top it off, I didn't fully understand all the concepts of the course. I was anxious and thought, *If I fail this exam, I could fail the course. If I fail this course, then I could fail out of college. If I flunk out of college, I will be working in our family construction business for the rest of my life.* While construction is a respectable profession, it was not my passion. My default conclusion was to work really hard.

For the next four and a half years, I took copious notes, read the chapters, focused on the material, and gave it just enough effort to graduate college with a 3.2 GPA and a BA in marketing. I did it! I was a college graduate, and now I would be set for life!

Three weeks later, I married my wife, Erica, and had a job locked-in making $30,000 a year. (That was a decent starting salary in 1998.) All in all, I had overcome my height deficit, my acne plague, my education challenge, and many other so-called setbacks to be an overcomer. Phew! I'm so glad that I had learned early on to pull my life up by the bootstraps, meet challenges head-on, and change my situations.

CHAPTER THREE | 30 WEEKS

In 2001, my wife, Erica, and I loved life. We had been married two years and were moving along life's path at the classic American pace. I had a degree in marketing, and Erica was pursuing a career as a midwife. We were deeply involved in our local church, had close, personal friends, and were ready to start having kids. We felt as though we had all the necessary life tools and were prepared for anything. Our life above the surface was beautiful, and anyone sailing by could easily admire the scenery of our life.

We found ourselves sitting in a doctor's corner office as sunshine beamed through the large windows. It was September 25, 2001, and we were getting the worst news of our life.

When expecting your first baby, you do not want to make an appointment with an obstetrician specializing in high-risk pregnancies. Erica is such a huge advocate of natural birth that she did not want to be in a doctor's office at all. A week prior, I made the decision that we were going to have a sonogram simply to confirm that our baby was right on schedule and that everything looked normal with no concerns. After all, Erica was almost eight months along, and we were planning to have the baby at home. It took her a year to convince me that a home birth was viable, so at a bare minimum, I wanted a clean bill of health.

I was working as the youth pastor at my home church, so we had to figure out a cheap way to have a sonogram performed. A friend of ours worked at the community college and let us know of their free sonogram program. That fit our budget! We were so excited about the procedure, and we decided that we did not want to know the sex of the baby. We only wanted to know the status of his or her health; and, of course, we were sure that it would be good.

About forty minutes into the sonogram, we started having concerns. The nursing students kept going in and out of the room. An instructor walked in to inspect the screen. They whispered to each other on the side, and finally, she said, "We do not see something that we should, and we would like you to see this doctor." She slipped us a piece of paper with the name of one of Austin's most well-known neonatal obstetricians scribbled on it. We called his office immediately and got an appointment that afternoon.

At that point, we were kicking ourselves for securing an appointment at the community college. "This was one time we should have splurged and gone to a real doctor. They are inexperienced and don't know much! They are students after all." we told ourselves. "We will visit the doctor's office. He will say that it was all a misunderstanding and the college had inferior equipment."

While we waited for the next appointment, I drove back to the church for a few hours. I stuck my head into the Senior Pastor's office, and he asked how the sonogram went. Nonchalantly, I mentioned the students' assessment, and we agreed I would go to the next appointment, and everything would be placed back in order.

Erica eagerly greeted me in the waiting room, rubbing her pregnant belly, as all good moms do. We walked into the examination room, and a competent, courteous technician completed the second sonogram. Then, the doctor entered, looked thoroughly at the baby, and asked us to follow him back to his office.

I am not sure if you have ever been to the principal's office, but this long walk felt very similar. Being asked to the doctor's office has to be one of the worst invitations you can receive.

We entered into the office and sat down. He looked across his desk and compassionately said, "Our concerns were confirmed with this sonogram. The 'something' that the community college had not seen was your baby's brain." He continued to say that our baby had severe hydrocephalus and would be born with serious birth defects.

In layman's terms, hydrocephalus is "water on the brain." This condition is caused when the natural fluid in the brain does not drain effectively. We all have fluid in our brain, but a healthy body drains the fluid at the perfect rate. Our child's fluid was not draining, and therefore, the brain was quite literally being forced out against our baby's skull. This fluid had severely limited the development of the brain, and our child would most likely be unable to talk, walk, or eat independently. In addition, there was a strong chance the baby would be deaf and blind.

Surgery was to immediately follow the birth, to install a shunt—a device that drains excess fluid off of the brain. As the doctor went on to explain the birth defect and prognosis, I felt as if I were dreaming. My head was spinning. I pinched my arm in hopes of waking up from a nightmare. Tears quietly streamed down Erica's cheeks. For the first fifteen minutes, I was in shock/denial. I wanted to walk out of the room and start all over again. Thoughts ricocheted against the walls of my finite mind at a thousand miles per hour, *Surely, you have this wrong. Let's try the sonogram again.*

At this point, I said, "Please tell us the sex of the baby. If we are traveling this path, we want to know everything about the baby." He managed to give us a little smile and say, "It's a girl."

Then, he gave us two options. The first option was to continue seeing him for weekly sonograms to monitor the baby's progress. We would also begin genetic testing to see if the problem was hereditary, and a Cesarean-section delivery would be scheduled around thirty-eight weeks of pregnancy.

Option two shocked us. The doctor said that if we chose not to continue the pregnancy, we could travel to Kansas for a late-term abortion. Only two or three states performed abortions after 30 weeks, and Texas was not one of them. After hearing both options, it took us moments to realize that we only had one option. We would be getting to know this Doc a whole lot better over the next few weeks.

We called our parents and our pastor. Thank God we had parents and a pastor on speed dial. (Back in 2001, there was still a thing called speed dial.) That first night we had dinner with my sister and her husband, who were also expecting their first child. I remember everything about that night. We ate pasta while sitting on the patio of The Brick Oven Restaurant. We slowly walked through all the details we could recall. It was a somber night, and yet it was incredibly comforting to have family to share the burden with us. After dinner, we returned home, and it all began to sink in. I went into the bathroom and shut the door. I slid down the wall and cried on the floor. I began to grieve the loss of our child. Not that she had died, but that our dreams of her future had died.

Many people called saying they were praying and that everything was going to be all right. "We are here with you. You can make it. You are not alone," they said.

Even after the initial tests, we had hopes that this would all go away. We thought we would pray, believe, and get the results we wanted. We faithfully attended each weekly sonogram with the anticipation of good news. Instead, the doctor gently informed us that our daughter's condition was worsening.

Several weeks after the initial diagnosis, our faith, our hope, our optimism eroded and were at a point of brokenness. We had lost every fiber of control. There was nothing we could do to change the problem.

Before the diagnosis, we were able to change our life situations with a little focus and hard work. If things were not going our way, we could pull life up by the bootstraps and get busy. Ultimately, over time, the situation at hand would change under the force of our persistence. Now, that was out of the question. Neither surgery nor therapy would fix this.

The relentless barrage of bad news plunged us way below the surface of our public, conscious life. As Christians, we sometimes feel that if our lives are not put together, we have failed at being a good person— we have failed God and those around us. It is tempting to "fake it until you make it." However, this was not a situation we could hide from the public and pretend as though everything was ok. Instead, this birth defect had the potential of wrecking everything. We faced the reality that our world was completely changing.

I could not grow taller, study harder, take better medicine, and practice more. I could not fix this. I could not implement the tried-and-true "work harder" formula I had been using to master my destiny.

I could do NOTHING.

I also could not stay above the waterline. For the first time in my existence, I felt I was being plunged below the surface of my life.

CHAPTER FOUR | HAPPY BIRTHDAY

We arrived at the doorstep of week thirty-eight and with it came the scheduled C-section delivery. Saturday, November 24, 2001, two days after Thanksgiving, Erica and I loaded the car early in the morning and took a nervous ride to Brackenridge Hospital. Our moms and dads were waiting there to greet us at the door. Kennady was to be the first grandchild for both sets of parents. While we waited for surgery, family members and church friends filtered through, offering prayers and advice. I sat with great anticipation and thought of all the possibilities.

I just knew that the doctor would deliver our baby girl, and there would be a miracle in the room. Everyone would be shocked as we saw our baby's completely healthy body enter the world. We would glorify God because of the miracle He had performed for us all. Final tests would scientifically confirm the great work that an all-knowing, all-powerful God had accomplished. Just then, a nurse peeked her head around the corner and said, "It's time to go!" Positioning herself as the wheelchair driver, she rolled Erica down the long hallway. The drama and delay began to crescendo with each rotation of the wheelchair across the linoleum flooring. I watched as the corridor narrowed, and Erica shrank out of sight.

My waiting continued until finally, I was called into the delivery room. I walked into a pristine, white room. Nurses and doctors worked around Erica. She was awake and able to squeak out a smile for me. I came to her side, and we whispered about how cold the room was. She was already prepped. Within a few quick moments, the doctor reached in and brought our daughter into the room.

The first moments of birth are life-changing—a flash of time every parent remembers forever. The first breaths, the first cry, the open eyes as they capture the hearts of everyone in the room. We looked in awe at the miracle of life—a distinct stand-alone frame in time—and in the next blink, our hearts sank a notch. We saw that her head was much larger than average.

I went straightaway to the small table where she was being tended to and began holding her hand and speaking to her. There was so much love between dad and baby girl at that moment. Standing there, I realized that my life was going to be different. I realized then that I needed to change my attitude, my expectations, and my prayers. My perspective needed to be shaped, not by my education or experience, but by how God was choosing to work through this child. Of course, all of those thoughts went un-articulated, but looking back, I see that moment at the bedside was monumental in the building of my faith. A day would come, not so far off, that my prayers, attitudes and expectations did indeed change.

That said, the worst was yet to come. The medical team sent our daughter immediately into the Neonatal Intensive Care Unit (NICU). The doctors wanted to perform an MRI early in the day to determine the extent of the birth defect. We all patiently waited and spoke with family members who were visiting the hospital. We were praying and believing for the MRI to show signs of healing. We just knew that it was only a matter of time before things would turn around. But, this was not the time.

Following the MRI, our neurosurgeon asked us to join him in the viewing room. He slid a few pictures of our daughter into the glass, and we put full trust in his analysis. However, when he began to talk, the dark room became a cave. He softly stated, "The condition is much worse than we expected." Our daughter did have hydrocephalus, but she also had a condition called alobar holoprosencephaly—commonly referred to as HPE. It meant that her brain not only had extra fluid, but it never separated into two lobes. Healthy people have a two-sided brain: right and left lobes. Our daughter only had one lobe, and no one knew if it was only the right, the left, or a combination of both in one.

Once again, two options were offered. We could allow her to continue life as she was, with fluid on her brain. In this scenario, Kennady's life would eventually end through natural causes. The second option was to perform a surgery that would drain the excess fluid from her brain through a VP shunt, thereby, permanently reducing the swelling. They could do nothing about the lack of separation in her lobes. In either case, the doctor said it could be anywhere from six months to two years before the condition finally took her life. Erica and I looked at each other and in unity said that we wanted to perform the shunt operation and give our baby any chance for life that we possibly could. Our faith in God and overall optimism did not allow us to give up so easily.

This mini-meeting with the brain surgeon was the lowest point for me. I remember walking out into the hallway and leaning up against the wall. My head fell back; I squeezed my eyes shut. My father walked up to me and stood by my side.

After a moment, I collected my thoughts and said, "Two things really bother me. First, this is not Kennady's fault; she had no option. She was just being herself and being born, yet this has happened to her! The second thing is that society will not value her as a normal person. They won't see that her soul and spirit are just as real and as normal as theirs. Most people will not take the time to look beyond the abnormal outer shell and see the innocent girl underneath. They will see a severely deformed young girl and immediately, subconsciously devalue her. That is not fair for her."

The reality of a daughter with special needs had finally sunk in. Erica's womb, along with my faith and prayer, had shielded me during the pregnancy. However, now that my daughter was out here with us, we were forced to accept the disability. Test result after test result answered our prayers with a self-evident "no," but we were always holding out hope for the next sonogram. After the sonograms failed to report the good news, we relied on her birth day. The birth brought another "NO." In the hallway that day, I was accepting the denial of my prayer request, and that was difficult. The plans and dreams that we had for our daughter were violently colliding with her reality.

There are so many lofty dreams imagined by first-time parents. While registering for baby shower gifts at the department store, you are thinking not only of room colors, clothing choices, and the latest baby gadgets, but you are daydreaming about the future. We conjured up ideas of college degrees, professions, spouses. Now, I had no dreams to dream.

WHY ME?

I never saw a wild thing feel sorry for itself. A small bird will drop frozen dead from a bough without ever having felt sorry for itself.

—David Herbert Lawrence

What is happening to my life? What is happening to my family? This certainly was not the future we had envisioned! After all, we were Christians, and I worked in full-time ministry helping kids in our local church! This type of thing didn't happen to people like me. In fact, my devotion to God went unbroken since my own birth! My mom was actually in a Sunday night church service when she went into labor with me. She handed my 2-year-old sister to some friends on the next pew and rushed to the hospital. I was born at 12:19 a.m., early Monday morning. Six days later, we were back on the same pew; this time I was in my mom's arms instead of her womb.

Since that weekend of my birth, I have not missed a Sunday service unless I was sick or out of town. And let me say that we had to be deathly ill before a sickness would permit us to miss a service. These days, you have to be free of a fever for twenty-four hours before people will allow you back in Sunday School. Back in the old days, if you were sick, you were supposed to go to church so the elders could lay hands on you and pray! You were a backslider if you weren't there every single week. It sounds a bit funny now, but that's how we rolled back then.

When we walked out of the doctor's office that warm September day, I could not fathom that the news about Kennady would be instrumental in shaping me into the person God wanted me to be.

Though it was intense, I am extremely thankful for my background that honored God at all costs. It has created habits in my life that have held me in uncertain times. However, the weakness in that religious system is that it left me and others vulnerable to developing entitlement attitudes in our hearts. Since I had performed such good works for God, I thought I would get a pass on all persecution.

I remember, just a couple months before this doctor visit, driving down the road and thinking, *I wonder what it would be like if my child were mentally disabled. Nah, that would never happen to me. That is like winning the "bad" lottery.* I immediately shelved that thought and said a little prayer like, "Lord, thanks that I don't have to go through things like that." All my life, I had seen the provision of God.

One of the most controversial parts of Jesus Christ's ministry was pointing out to the religious leaders that their hearts were becoming corrupt in the midst of what looked so holy on the outside. Isaiah prophesied it, and Jesus reaffirmed it in Matthew when he said, "These people honor me with their lips, but their heart is far from me." (Mathew 15:8 New Living Translation)

This scripture offers a lot more depth than my application here, but, suffice it to say, I had fallen into the same trap as these religious leaders. I found my identity in my works and not in the grace of God. When my identity was wrapped up in my actions, I was setting myself up for failure. In future chapters, I will discuss this in detail and also talk about the accountability that kept me from going too far down this disastrous path.

As I mentioned before, Kennady's diagnosis plunged Erica and me way below the surface of our visible life. We were no longer simply dealing with what color we were going to paint her room or what kind of stroller we wanted to use. Instead, we faced new challenges: *How are we going to make it? Is God going to fix this? How can we still have a good life if this is our new reality?*

These are deep issues that, pre-birth, we did not have to contemplate seriously. Now, there was no option. We were being forced to play the dealt hand, and we were coming to terms with life's most serious questions. *Who is God? Who are we? Who is Kennady?*

CHAPTER FIVE | DOCTOR SAID, "NO MEANING"

Kennady spent the next six weeks in the Neonatal Intensive Care Unit (NICU) including: Christmas, New Year's Day, and the day the University of Texas played the Big 12 Championship Game. (Those are big days in Austin, TX!) She had tubes hooked up everywhere. Machines were blinking stats to hospital staff. Nurses were walking around, and there were about 30 other babies in cribs very close by. We had to wear gowns and face masks to protect the infants from potential illness. Fortunately, each bed had a rocking chair, so at least one parent could sit and rock their baby.

The NICU is not known for its homey atmosphere or welcoming décor. Unfortunately, it is either dark and cold or fluorescent bright white and cold. Either way, it is lousy lighting and chilly. We spent hours in those cold rooms feeding her a bottle, rocking her to sleep, singing songs, and introducing her to new friends and family, one person at a time. Visitors had to put on a gown and a face mask and then scrub their hands for 3 minutes before winding through the cribs to see our little miracle.

Christmas morning marked our thirtieth day in the NICU. Instead of sitting around a beautiful tree and opening gifts with extended family, Erica and I dressed Kennady as a little red elf. We sat around her hospital crib and thought of what life would be like when we left the hospital. We had ridden the roller coaster of emotion. *Our daughter is born! What a miracle! She has a horrible diagnosis. She is recovering well! She looks different than healthy babies.* We were up and down. Up and down.

One unforgettable day, I was visiting with Kennady by her crib. At the foot of the bed was a clipboard of doctor notes. Back in 2001, it was typical to leave a chart at the crib so doctors and nurses on other shifts could stay apprised of the patient's situation. However, on this day, my sideways glance caught the last line of the progress report. In the doctor's hand, it read, *"the parents understand that there is no chance of their daughter having a meaningful life."*

The bang of those words rang in my mind like a gavel strike. Judgment passed over my daughter's entire life with a short, yet sweeping, sentence. I was utterly crushed and, seconds later, angry. I thought, *My daughter has meant more to me in the last two days than you will ever mean to me.* I was furious. The indifference! The audacity! Suddenly his credentials, his education, his years of training were meaningless to me, just as my daughter was meaningless to him.

For ten years, I thought about that moment at the crib

and always wanted to go look up Kennady's medical records to see if they reflect that statement still. I wanted proof. I had almost convinced myself that I misread it. Undoubtedly, the transcriber would have edited the comment to read more appropriately. In fact, one time we mentioned it to our palliative care doctor, and she could not believe that a doctor said that.

So, in early 2011, I went through the process of accessing Kennady's records. They told me that it would take several weeks to get the documents, and then I could come to the hospital to find the correct record. Kennady was in the hospital for forty-two days during that period. You can imagine how many pages of records that included. I finally received the call that the documents were ready, and I scheduled an appointment to review them.

Erica dropped me off at the front door of the hospital and waited outside for me to run in and get them. My emotions began to swell as I walked the same stark halls as I had a decade before. I was nervous and excited all at the same time. The clerk took a few minutes and then returned with a large folder of documents. It was about four inches thick. Fortunately, the information I was looking for was close to the top. I turned page 6 of the records and saw this:

PROBLEM #2: PSYCHOSOCIAL INTERVENTION
Onset: 11/25/2001.

Diagnosis of hydrocephalus made prenatally. Parents met with Dr. Wilson prior to delivery. Dr. Hodges met with the family prior to and after delivery, reviewing the patient's condition and treatment plans. They were well read and have a very good understanding. All questions answered. Dr. Wilson met with the family 11/25 and reviewed the devestating defect or injury revealed by the MRI. The parents understand that there is no changce of their daughter having a meaningful life.

Tears fell down my face. I couldn't believe it. There it was. First of all, the statement in the report was incorrect. Erica and I never expressed the understanding that our daughter's life was meaningless. That is what was so disturbing. It was like they were saying we agreed with them. Wrong. False. Untrue.

At this point, I think it is important that I clarify a few things. The doctors and nurses did a phenomenal job physically caring for our daughter in the NICU. We are incredibly grateful for their hard work. We also do not believe the doctor was intentionally trying to be mean in his assessment of Kennady's life. It merely was a clear sign that our doctor, like many others, was tangled in the entrapping lies of society that define meaning with skewed and perverted definitions.

I stood up from the table, slid the big stack of papers back, and asked the attendant to make a copy of that one piece of paper. I am sure that the rest of the documents contained valuable information about Kennady's care; however, at this point, all that information seemed worthless. The attendant graciously made a copy, and I walked out of the office. I trekked back down the stark halls. I made it back to the minivan at the hospital entrance. The three kids were in the van with Erica, laughing, talking and in their world. I got in the passenger door and just sat there. Erica said, "Well, what did you find?" To which, I flatly replied, "It was there," and then handed her the copy.

Erica and I often wondered what our daughter would have to accomplish before the doctor would deem her meaningful. If she could walk, would she cross the threshold of meaning? If she was able to form words or write sentences, would she be meaningful? Would she have a high market value if she were able to go to college or get married?

I sat in the car, looking at that piece of paper and found myself asking the same question, facing the same issue, coming back to the same existential chasm that I encountered when I looked into Sammy's eyes and asked him, "Can you be deaf and still be whole." Except, this time, I was asking it of my daughter.

PART TWO | How to BE Whole

CHAPTER SIX

GOING DEEP

In the summer of 1910, an enormous chunk of ice fell from the western cliffs of Greenland and floated south, bobbing up and down in the Labrador Sea. Every year the Ilulissat ice-shelf loses large masses of ice, forming a labyrinth of icebergs. Most melt when they meet the Gulf Stream at its feeding point into the Atlantic Ocean. However, this particular berg was over a mile long and had the mass to make the journey into the Atlantic. By April of 1912, it melted significantly, yet it still stood seventy-five feet above the water, boasting a breadth of approximately 400 feet, plunged over 700 feet below the surface, and weighed more than 75 million tons. Within days this would become the most famous iceberg of all time.

On a dark, frigid, icy night, the mighty Titanic struck this ice mountain in the North Atlantic Ocean. At the time, the Titanic was the largest ship in the world and thought to be unsinkable. It turns out, icebergs are serious business and not a match for even the largest ships. The great collision cost 1,500 lives and changed sea navigation forever. From that point in history, every sailor looked for, planned for, and routed for icebergs. Teams of people were formed to patrol the oceans and report sightings, sizes, and coordinates for the foreboding ice mountains. In short, icebergs changed the game.

As you may know, icebergs are deceiving. Only 10 percent of one is visible. Ninety percent of the iceberg is under the surface of the water. When sailors cruise across the ocean, their calculations must factor in the most significant part of the berg—the part you cannot see—the part that matters most!

THE TIP OF THE ICEBERG

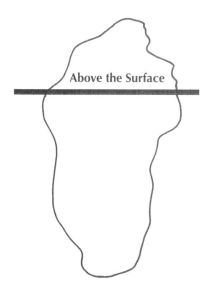

In the morning, many of us get up, get dressed, fix our hair, and make ourselves presentable for society. We walk out the door and show the world the "tip of the iceberg." Our characteristics above the waterline—our vocabulary, car, favorite brands, style, body mass index, hobbies, social media posts, occupation, credentials, and experiences—become the ice mountain that everyone sailing by can see. We buy into the lie that our wholeness comes from the visible part of our lives. And so, we spend most of our time, money, and energy maintaining what meets the eye. We believe that if we can fit these features within the norms of society, then we will be successful, accomplished, approved, and accepted.

Life is exhausting when we spend all of our energy

investing in the 10 percent. Neglecting the 90 percent can be destructive. Pastor Pete Scazzero clearly describes the iceberg/hidden-life concept. He wrote:

When we deny our pain, losses, and feelings year after year, we become less and less human. We transform slowly into empty shells with smiley faces painted on them. But when I begin to allow myself to feel a wider range of emotions, including sadness, depression, fear, and anger, a revolution in my spirituality is unleashed.

(*Emotionally Healthy Spirituality,* 2006)

Below the surface, in a watery suspension, our emotions, memories, experiences, values, paradigms, history, dreams, self-image, and beliefs swirl in existence.

LEVEL ONE BELOW THE SURFACE—OUR MISTAKES

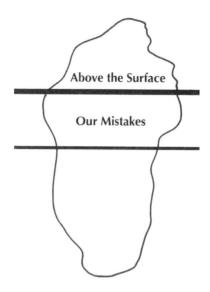

Above the Surface

Our Mistakes

Just under the surface of our public lives lie the actions that we are not proud of, but we do not think they are that big of a deal. These are our mistakes and mess-ups. Last night's argument with your spouse. Last week when you stared at the college co-ed jogging down the road. Last year when you did not report all your income on your tax return. Last decade when you were not completely honest on the job interview.

We do not post these types of things on social media. Why not? We want people to think that we are not this way. We want to portray to people that we are ethical and moral individuals. These are examples of the mistakes we do not believe are game-changers. We feel like we could change them at any time. They are not addictive behaviors or habits that control us. We justify them, thinking that they did not harm anyone. We assume everyone deals with these types of issues, and they are simply something that humans go through. However, while small, they are big enough that we hide them just below the surface.

LEVEL TWO BELOW THE SURFACE—OUR PAIN

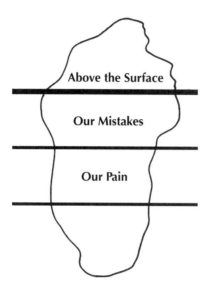

As we dive deeper below the surface, we see more substantial issues, actions, and regrets that reside in our mind and soul. These are not particular instances, but overall feelings and weight that we carry. These painful emotions are a result of activities in which we have willing participated, along with actions that have happened to us.

We deal with the guilt of making bad decisions. We also deal with the pain of being a victim. Since we do not want people to know about these issues, we hide them away from public knowledge. We do not want them to define us, and we vow that someday we will process through them, but not today. For example, it would make us uneasy if others were aware of our discontent with our career path. What would people think if they knew about our feeling of failure from dropping out of college? Here is where guilt resides. Here is where we harbor the failure of losing weight, gaining weight, being single, not having kids, having rebellious kids, and on the list goes.

Many of us craft jokes to deal with these issues if they ever pop up in general conversation. It goes something like this: "Hey John, you still working that job at the distribution center? How long have you been there? 120 years?" You respond, "Ha! Yeah, I'm going for the record. If I stay another 30 years, I get the Energizer Bunny Award!" Outwardly, you give a chuckle and a bad joke. Inwardly, you want to punch them in the throat and quit your job. We use humor to hide the pain these failures have created. The laugh gets you past the moment of focus, but it never effectively heals the core issue.

At this level, we also deal with the pain that others have caused us. Many carry the weight of childhood abuse, a spouse who abandoned the marriage, a business partner who took the money and left you with the debt, or a church that did you wrong. Situations like these cut significant wounds into our soul. We sequester them well below the surface of public knowledge for several reasons. We believe we are the only ones who have gone through this particular situation. We do not think others would see us the same after it is shared, or we think that we caused the situation. As a result, we pack them away and think that maybe we will address them later.

LEVEL THREE BELOW THE SURFACE— OUR VIEW OF OUR SELF AND GOD

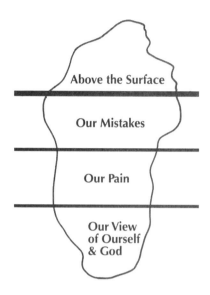

Above the Surface

Our Mistakes

Our Pain

Our View
of Ourself
& God

As we keep diving miles below the surface of our public life, we finally get to the most fundamental and essential aspects of who we are. Our feelings towards God, our core belief about who God is, what God does, and if He genuinely cares about us, all live at this level. Here reside the deep roots of faith, doubt, wins, losses, and traumas. Do we believe that God loves us? Do we trust that we are a son or daughter of God? Who are we? What is our identity? Deeply seated in this part of our lives are the truths and lies that we believe about God and, consequently, about ourselves.

There is a direct relationship between this deepest level and all of the others already mentioned. This deepest space either sends energy and confidence for dealing with the other levels, or it sends confusion and weakness. What everyone sees in our outward appearance and behavior is intricately connected to this intimate, sub-visible level of our being.

In the late 19th century, French psychologist Pierre Janet was one of the first people to make a connection between someone's past and his or her present-day situation. He coined the word "subconscious" (Ellenberger, 1970). Miles below the surface of our public life, lie the events of our past, the people who have shaped us, and our formal and informal education. These create our framework of processing life in the present. Not only do people rarely want to discuss these factors with others, but most never want to think about them privately either. We are so focused on the outward appearance that we suppress these thoughts and feelings, thinking that ignoring them will make them insignificant.

In John chapter 5, Jesus offered wholeness to a sick, disabled man at the community pool. Jesus asked the exasperated man, "Wilt thou be made whole?" (John 5:6 KJV) In other words, "Would you like to be made whole?" Our first reaction, most likely, is to believe that Jesus healing the man's crippled legs would deliver the wholeness he desired. However, wholeness encapsulates so much more than an "above the surface" healing. Wholeness means that we have complete inner peace *below the surface of our lives.*

For thirty-eight years, this man had not only faced a physical disability but also the deep emotional and psychological suffering of separation from society. The story says people had continually cheated and taken advantage of him. Think of how these experiences formed this man's perception of himself and God deep in the recesses of his heart.

Jesus made this man whole. As the story reads, he touched the surface and healed the man's legs. However, for wholeness to be delivered, he could not have stopped there. I believe Jesus' divine healing traveled beyond the muscles and bones and reached below the surface, into this man's heart. I believe that Jesus affirmed that his identity was no longer "crippled man" or "left behind." Jesus affirmed that this man was loved, forgiven, and never needed to look elsewhere for worth. His body (what people saw), his soul and spirit (what people sensed) all began to operate with an accurate perception of God and who he was in Jesus.

Here is some really good news. As the deepest parts of us start healing, the effect works its way up to the surface of our lives. We focus less on our outside appearance—the visible part of our lives. We worry less with reworking ourselves to fit the norm. We begin to function at our best as the deepest levels of sub-consciousness rest in a firm belief of who God is and who we are in Him. We begin to experience wholeness as the truth works its way up through the higher levels of our lives. The work of transformation addresses the injustices of our past and redeems each episode of sin, rebellion, hurt or failure in our lives. Our temptation to appease the crowd dies away, and our confidence is rooted in Jesus.

OUR LIFE PACE

Why do we not simply get to the bottom of who we are, deal with it, become healthy, and then move on to conquer life? Our lives progress at such a rapid pace that we struggle to find the time or desire to address the deeper parts of our lives. We are too busy with what is pressing directly in front of us to invest time in the abstract. We think, *If I can just make it to the weekend, I'll deal with it then.* The weekend comes, and we binge on our favorite pastime because every minute of every day is filled with work, entertainment, social media, taking care of kids, exercise, eating, sleeping, and repeating it all.

| CHAPTER SEVEN | WHO ARE YOU? |

To be, or not to be, that is the question.
—Hamlet, Act III, Scene I, William Shakespeare

As I begin to write this chapter, I am thankful to report that our daughter, Kennady, recently celebrated her 18th birthday. For almost two decades now, she has been defying the odds. The prognosis of her life only being several months has been thoroughly obliterated. However, Kennady's life looks quite a bit different from you and me.

She is unable to walk or talk. Because she is unable to eat by mouth, we have to feed her by a tube that connects directly to her stomach. She usually takes around ten prescriptions daily, and someone is required to care for all her needs. Over the years, Erica and I have learned a lot about the medical field and, at times, think we could go to work for a hospital. Kennedy's condition has required her to have a neurologist, a pulmonologist, an ophthalmologist, an endocrinologist, an orthopedist, and several other specialists. She has had several surgeries to help with her muscles, intestines, and spine.

Amid all these daunting realities that Kennedy lives with, she is the happiest 12th grader you have ever seen in a wheelchair. She speaks to us with a contagious smile. One thing that is extremely healthy and normal for her is the ability to communicate through emotion. She alerts us when she is in pain by crying a certain way. She informs us that she is tired of a television show by growling a certain way. She signals that she is pleased, happy, content, or excited by smiling, giggling, or laughing hysterically.

She loves bouncy rides on the four-wheeler and the slow rumble of a school bus. Your heart will melt when you take her by the hand, and she looks into your eyes. She doesn't know about the tension in the Middle East. She has never met a stranger and has no clue that people stare in the grocery store.

When you see Kennady and her family, it is quite clear that she has had a profound and meaningful life. Kennady is meaningful, yet she cannot do much of anything. Kennady's body is broken in many ways, yet her soul and spirit seem to be more whole than anyone we know. Through the span of her life, we have learned a lot about wholeness.

Wholeness is about BEING.

"To be" is such a powerful verb. I remember taking Spanish 1 in high school. Verbs were challenging to learn because of the many conjugations. There was a different pronunciation depending on the tense and the subject of the sentence. The very first word we learned in Spanish was "to be." Why? We learned this verb first because everything in existence hinges around this verb. Not only important in Spanish, but in all languages and all realms of life, "to be" establishes everything.

What are you? Who are you? I am. She is. He was. We were. They have been. I will be.

These are all examples of the "to be" verbs and their tenses. At the root of "to be" verbs is our identity. Who are we as a person? What are we as a group? Think about this dynamic concept: We call our species human *beings*. We are beings. At a deep philosophical level, this means that we are defined as entities that exist. We are defined by who we are, by being. So, the question is, who are you being? Who have you been? Who will you be?

As I have mentioned in previous chapters, the human race continually defines each other by many factors, none of which are merely being someone. Our number one way to categorize people is by what they DO. Think about it. What is the third question you ask a new acquaintance? 1. What is your name? 2. Are you from around here? 3. What do you do for a living? We naturally want to ask someone what they do because it is an easy question and answer for most people—not too personal or risky. However, we also subconsciously wish to categorize this person on a scale. We want to see how we match up to them. The answer to what they do gives us a ton of information in two or three words.

Occupations and education levels tell us if someone is a hard worker, disciplined or lazy. It tells us if they have connections to other people. It tells us if they have access to money. We begin to wonder if we can leverage this relationship for our gain, or we possibly feel confident because this person has not been able to achieve all that we have. Occasionally, we meet people with a well-known, prominent last name, and we realize that this person has power because of their family's clout. We are tempted to value them based on what that power can provide to us. We draw their meaning based on our perception of what they have accomplished: career, education, and ability to manage their resources, network, etc.

This way of ascribing meaning to each other is not God's original intention. When God created Adam and Eve, they existed in the garden as images of God. They had unique characteristics, but those were valuable because they reflected God's glory. They did not receive any value or meaning because of something they came up with on their own.

Everything begins to fall apart for Adam and Eve (and the rest of us humans) when they listen to the serpent's offering. He tells them that who they are is not good enough. He says that what they have accomplished is not sufficient, and he offers them more. Before this temptation, Adam and Eve were content simply being God's kids. They were not seeking more power or knowledge. They were not even hungry for the actual fruit. However, when the serpent tempted them with more power and knowledge, merely BEING Adam and Eve was not enough. Now they needed to add something to their existence. At this point, people lost their contentment with simply being.

When God begins his path of redemption for humanity, He goes back to the original plan. He identifies a group of humans as "His people." Starting with Abraham and Sarah, God identifies Israelites as special simply because of WHO they are.

The Lord said to Abram:

Leave your native country, your relatives, and your father's family, and go to the land that I will show you. I will make you into a great nation. I will bless you and make you famous, and you will be a blessing to others. I will bless those who bless you and curse those who treat you with contempt. All the families on earth will be blessed through you.

(Genesis 12:1–3)

God tells Abram to leave all that has defined him. He is to leave his homeland and family and be redefined entirely by God. God changes his name from Abram to Abraham to signify the complete identity revolution that is happening. God's instructions are big, yet they are not complicated. In Genesis 17:4, God tells Abraham that He will make him the father of multiple nations. In essence, *I will BE your God, and you will BE my people.* The entire covenant is about identity between God and Abraham and his descendants.

From this point forward, the Israelites are known as "God's people." They are to be the vehicle for God's salvation for all people. Through them, God speaks to the world. Through the Jewish bloodline, God brings a Savior who will redeem every broken part of the earth, every creature, and every person. However, all this meaningfulness rests NOT on the Jews' ability to save the world. It is entirely reliant on them simply being God's people and allowing God to work through them. If you have studied Israel's plight through history, you know they have failed countless times to represent God. However, God never abandons the plan. God knows that their identity of being His people is enough.

If we fast forward to the beginning of the New Testament, we see a God who continues to love the world deeply, yet His people have lost their identity. There is so much confusion and turmoil. This text says it so clearly:

But with eager hope, the creation looks forward to the day when it will join God's children in glorious freedom from death and decay. For we know that all creation has been groaning as in the pains of childbirth right up to the present time. (Romans 8:21–22)

Well aware of this groaning, God is about to transform everything and everyone when He enters the world as one of us—Jesus, the Son of God. Through Jesus, God will renew the earth literally from the ground up. Every creature, plant, and person can participate and reflect God's beauty. Just as He has from the beginning of time, in this move of God, He continues to identify His people.

We see this taking shape in the New Testament when John baptizes Jesus. As Jesus comes out of the waters of baptism, a voice from heaven says, "...This is my dearly loved Son, who brings me great joy" (Matthew 3:17). At this point, Jesus has not taught a sermon, healed a blind eye, or died for the sins of the world. He was God's Son and brought great joy BEFORE he did the massive work of salvation. As he leaves the Jordan River that day, he begins his public ministry standing on the foundation of BEING someone and belonging to someone. All of his meaning (and obedience) stems from his identity.

Unfortunately, most of us do the opposite. We try to find our identity by what we do, what we like or dislike, how we dress, what groups we relate to, etc. We do good, obedient things to be approved by God. We want His favor, so we exert an excessive amount of time and energy striving to be in good standing with God. When we are nailing it as a Christian, we feel terrific about ourselves. We feel like we are in good standing with God and, therefore, His son or daughter. When we are doing well, we are tempted to take the credit for our good behavior, and we look down on those who are not holding their end of the bargain. In reverse, when we are struggling to live a righteous life with constant mess-ups, we regularly beat ourselves up. We live in guilt and explore ways to pay penance for our sin. In these moments, we feel God is far from us, and we do not deserve to be His son or daughter. We feel less meaningful.

In both of the above scenarios, our performance determines our sense of meaning or self-worth. If we were to define this way of life in a word, it would be "pride." The Bible teaches us that pride is when we take a self-centered approach to life and evaluate everything from our point of view. The Bible warns us about this approach: "For the world offers only a craving for physical pleasure, a craving for everything we see, and pride in our achievements and possessions. These are not from the Father but are from this world." (1 John 2:16)

God offers you a better way where your performance does not determine your sense of meaning. Just as Jesus was identified as God's Son at His baptism before He offered any supernatural performance, you too can be defined as God's child before you obey Him with any great zeal. The Gospel of Jesus Christ offers you identity as God's child right now, as you are. God wants you in His family (the same family as Abraham and the original Jews). God wants you as a part of His chosen people. Right now.

Our first response to this is often something similar to this: *How in the world is that possible? How could I possibly be accepted by God before I do anything good? How could I be a part of God's holy people before I can stop doing bad things?*

That seems so implausible. Surely, I need to clean myself up. Surely, I need to make myself presentable and eligible to be in His family. It seems cheap for me to sort of jump in the back door of His family without doing anything first.

These are all excellent questions. When we ask these questions, it is a good sign because it shows that we understand the holiness of God and the brokenness of man. However, it also indicates that we do not truly understand the power of Jesus Christ. God is entirely perfect, and we are the opposite. We do not deserve to be with God in any circumstance. Yet, God loves us so much that He did not want to be separated from us for eternity.

How do broken, messed up people become a part of God's holy family? Jesus is the answer to this great puzzle. Jesus comes to earth and lives the ultimate life as a Son of God. In other words, Jesus lives a life that is worthy of BEING God's Son. In essence, He lives the life that we all desire to live. We keep messing it up. Jesus never messed it up. Not only does Jesus never sin, but in His death, burial, and resurrection, He fulfills all of the work needed for you and me to BE in the family. Earlier I said that we feel it may be cheap to sort of jump into the family of God without doing anything. Actually, it is not cheap at all. The price of adoption into God's chosen family is extremely expensive, and that is what makes Jesus so incredibly amazing.

Just before Jesus' death on the cross, he meets with his disciples in the upper room and offers them a new deal.

As they are eating dinner together, Jesus says, "Don't let your hearts be troubled. Trust in God, and trust also in me. There is more than enough room in my Father's home... I am the way, the truth, and the life. No one can come to the Father except through me" (John 14:1–2,6).

Basically, He is saying, "You have a seat at the Father's table if you trust that I am who I say I am and if you believe in what I have done for you."

When we give Jesus credit for accomplishing the complete work, or debt, for our right standing with God, we are choosing to deny the credit for ourselves. When we trust that Jesus Christ did all of the work necessary for us to be a son or daughter of God, then our pride melts away. We are completely out of the picture. When we rest in Jesus' accomplishment for our salvation, then we rest in our identity as a child of God. We no longer strive to accomplish it ourselves. Ultimately, we will be cheerfully obedient, and our lives will begin to reflect God's holiness, not because we are scared of losing our salvation, but because we are anchored in God's love for us. We know who we are way down below the surface of public opinion.

This is an excellent beginning of our faith and relationship with God. When we return to our original state of human BEING instead of human-doing, our meaning and, therefore, our sense of wholeness, comes from who we are, not what we do. This is one of the profound lessons that Erica and I have learned from our

daughter. Kennady is awesome at being a "human being."
She is awful at being a "human doing."

As we live with and care for our daughter, we find this
powerful truth to be gloriously contagious. We love our
daughter for who she is. We know that God loves her for
who she is. If God loves her in her state of disability, then
we know His love for us is not dependent on our level of
ability. God loves us all. It is time that we find wholeness
in being a child of God, being accepted by God, and being
comfortable with God's plan for our lives.

CHAPTER EIGHT

WHOLENESS IS ABOUT BEING ACCEPTED BY GOD

Trust in the Lord with all your heart,
and do not lean on your own understanding.

—Proverbs 3:5

Beginning with my childhood, I have craved the attention and approval of my parents. I have amazing parents. Wow! They raised me with incredible love, a perfect balance of affection and discipline. I never wanted to let them down and did my best to ensure their continued approval of me.

Throughout high school and college, I was "the good guy" in school. I never went to parties, drank, smoked, fill in the blank with whatever bad thing, I did not do it. I was not even tempted to do it. I helped lead the Fellowship of Christian Athletes club in high school. After graduating, I immediately began serving in our youth ministry. By the time I was 20, I was the primary youth leader at our church. I was also attending Texas State University, which was known by most as the biggest party school in Texas. I never went to a party in college. Every day, I was either studying at school or spending my time at the church working with our youth.

Over time, I began to take pride in my achievements at school and church. I would look at others my age and be critical of their journey. With a self-righteous attitude, I would think, *If they tried harder, they would not be in this place. If they had more discipline, they would not make those mistakes. Why can't they be more like me?* I never actually told anyone those things and did not consciously think in those particular terms. However, looking back on it, I now see how this attitudinal pattern began to evolve.

My good track record was building my image and my sense of wholeness. The older I got, and the longer I kept the track record good, I got a ton of positive feedback from friends, family, church leaders. I was even getting positive feedback from people in the community. I also believed that God must be really proud of me. After all, I had done Him a solid favor by acting the way I did (at least this was my perception). As the years passed, I kept working hard at the image, and it grew bigger and bigger. It also seemed more and more difficult to maintain. I found myself striving to hear more positive feedback.

As good as young Robin was, he was still a human. The truth is that I did sin. As you can tell, below the surface of my life, pride was growing. I was building a sort of "Tower of Babel" to myself. Pride was a dark condition of my heart. Above the surface of my life, my weakness was my attraction to girls. I dated a lot of girls, most of them Christian girls in the church. I always tried my hardest to end each relationship positively and remain friends with each one of them. You know, I am "the good guy." I tried my hardest to maintain a healthy physical boundary while dating. In my heart, I knew that a sexual relationship was reserved for marriage. At one point, during college, I fell. This was a crushing blow for me. I was devastated. I felt guilty that I had let down God and myself.

Because I had put so much effort into building my image above the surface, and I received so many accolades for being a good person, I could not talk to anyone. I was isolated from finding help because I could not face the people that meant so much to me. I could not imagine what would happen if people knew about this situation. What would happen to my position at church? What would my parents think? I could not bear the thought of these consequences, so I prayed and decided to keep it all to myself.

Thankfully, I had a mentor in my life who noticed something was going on and began to pry so much that I eventually confessed to him. He led me through that particular incident, and I progressed to a new chapter in life. I wish I could say that my facade was over at that point, and I never dealt with it again. Unfortunately, it would be years later before I found true wholeness, and my need for approval was satisfied.

Eventually, I became a pastor; our church began to grow quickly, and I found pleasure in people recognizing its success. As a pastor, my busiest day of the week is by far Sunday. I wake up around 5:15 a.m. and immediately begin my routine of prayer, meditation on the message, breakfast (oatmeal and eggs every day), black coffee, get dressed and go to church around 7:15 a.m. We currently have three services in the morning, so I worship and preach (x3), greet people, and put out fires until around 1:30 p.m. By the end of that whirlwind, I am completely exhausted. My family sometimes goes to eat after church with a few people. By 3 p.m., I usually fall on the bed and take a nap. For years, the nap has been followed by something really strange: depression.

I would wake from the nap and begin to feel depressed about the day. It did not matter if the church was full, we baptized people, or had all the volunteers we needed; I felt empty inside. This happened for years, and it made me hate Sunday nights. During football season, I would watch Sunday Night Football and try to forget about my feelings. When it was not football season, I would start surfing Facebook and Instagram to see what people were saying about Sunday morning's services. I was trolling for positive comments about the service and, most importantly, me. I wanted desperately to see pictures and comments on how the service helped them.

I wanted to hear about how well I preached and how people's lives were changed because of what I had done. Consciously, (above the surface) I wanted to give God the glory for a great day. Subconsciously, (below the surface) I desperately needed to be affirmed and accepted by my congregation.

Some days I would scroll through my feed and not see any feedback from that morning. Instead of simply logging off and going about my day, I needed more. I felt like I needed to stimulate the conversation about the morning, so I would post my own picture about the day and bait people to comment about how it was for them. Most of the time, I would get a few comments that would soothe my feelings for the moment. When they did not suffice, I would go to my wife and ask her, "Hey, what did you think about church today? What did you think of the message today?"

I was not whole.

A few years ago, I began diving way below the surface of my life. This intentional discipleship process revealed many areas where I craved approval in my life. Over a couple of years, I saw the different areas where I was not trusting in God's approval of me, and I was either striving for His approval or looking to people to fulfill that void. Because people often complimented me, and I was reasonably successful at what I did, I received a fair amount of positive reinforcement from people and felt that God must be proud of what I had accomplished.

This routine of hunting down the approval and finding it in little doses was like getting a hit off of a drug. Each little high was enough to make me feel good enough. In reality, I had learned to live on a substitute grace for years. In essence, I had nullified God's grace by looking to and accepting an alternative.

When we read the first couple chapters of the Bible, it is clear that God creates us in His image and that humans have a distinct connection to Him and each other. He has hard-wired us for a relationship with Him.

Adam and Eve were accepted by God in the garden and were satisfied in their relationship with Him. God gave them a desire for acceptance that He was perfectly fitted to fill. The problem came when the devil lied to Eve, and she believed that God was not enough. Like Eve, each one of us has been chasing after a cheap substitute. The solution is not to deny the need for approval, but face The One, turn towards The One, walk toward The One, The One that approves us already.

Believe it or not, Peter had the same problem as you and me. He often struggled with God's approval and people's acceptance. We know that Jesus accepted him as a disciple when Peter was a very rough fisherman. Peter was the first to declare that Jesus was the Christ, the Son of God. He walked on water. However, Peter was also the one who denied Jesus when Jesus was at the point of His greatest need and facing imminent death.

Then, Peter was forgiven and given a new chance. He preached a powerful message on the day of Pentecost, and 3,000 people were added to the church that day. The very next chapter in Acts tells us that Peter and John healed a man who was crippled for years. Peter is on track with the gospel message during these moments.

However, later, in the book of Galatians, we see Peter struggle with his need for approval once again. Peter had been hanging out with the Gentiles and feeling good about it. However, when the Jewish believers came back into town, Peter immediately distanced himself from the Gentiles because, "he was **afraid** of **criticism** from these people who insisted on the necessity of circumcision" (Galatians 2:12 emphasis mine).

Peter's need for approval by the religious leaders of the day dictated how he lived his life. This time, the apostle Paul called him out on it. Paul went on to say in his letter to the Galatians that Peter's hypocrisy caused people to be led astray. So, let's get this straight, Peter went from preaching a message in which 3,000 people were added to the church, to people leaving the church because of his example. Peter needed redirection, and that is why Paul called him out in front of everyone.

Peter's desire to please other people and earn their approval caused him to operate out of fear. **When we crave the approval of people over God's approval then we set ourselves up for fear and anxiety.** This lifestyle of fear caused Peter to be unproductive and even destructive to the work of God in his life. Paul would say later that we, in essence, nullify or frustrate the grace of God in our lives when we operate out of fear (Galatians 2:21). When we are afraid of people not liking us, we are handcuffing God's graciousness in our lives.

The fact is, we cannot please everyone. No matter how hard we try, we will experience rejection in some form. Peter worked hard to have the Jewish believers' approval, but we can be assured that they would have found something wrong anyway. You and I are in the same boat. We will never be able to please everyone. There will always be someone whose approval we cannot get.

In our family, we had to come to terms with the fact that our daughter would not be like other girls her age. When Kennady was a baby, no one noticed that she had special needs. She looked like any other baby. However, when she failed to hit the usual benchmarks for toddlers, we started getting stares. She was unable to walk and would make strange sounds or facial expressions. People would stop at the grocery store and stare. Little kids would come up and ask, "What happened to your baby?"

At this point, we were face to face with what the doctor unaffectionately stated about her meaning. "Their daughter will not have a meaningful life" could actually be translated to: "Their daughter will not be like others," or, "Others will not accept their daughter." As her parents, we immediately made the distinction that her value was not predicated on what others thought. Kennady's meaning would not be founded on her ability to fit in with everyone else. We could not seek out everyone else's approval for Kennady to be whole.

One of the most inspirational aspects of Kennady's existence is that she fully rests in her acceptance. She never struggles with the thought that we do not love her or accept her. She never thinks about the possibility that God does not love her. Kennady has not spent a second of her life doubting her value or meaning. Of course, her limited brain capacity contributes to this, but what a great disability! What if we could not possibly doubt our acceptance from God? What if we trusted completely that God accepts us, and that is all that matters?

I don't know about you, but I long to rest in this place of peace. It should not take a significant disability or diagnosis in our lives for us all to come to this powerful conclusion. The more I trust God's acceptance of me, the more peace pours into my life. I begin to rest in God's peace. Paul declares this to us in this passage:

Don't worry about anything; instead, pray about everything. Tell God what you need, and thank him for all he has done. Then you will experience God's peace, which exceeds anything we can understand. His peace will guard your hearts and minds as you live in Christ Jesus. (Philippians 4:6–7)

In another chapter, I will talk much more about the power of prayer in this equation, but for now, grasp the truth of peace guarding your heart and mind.

Our culture has a hard time resting from anything. We are always on the move. Merriam-Webster's defines rest as "(v): *to cease from action or motion: refrain from labor or exertion.*" I am sure the first thing that comes to mind when considering rest is our daily routine, work, and personal time. However, I am referring to the power of resting in a position of grace. **Instead of frantically moving and pressing to earn grace through your labor or exertion, God is calling you to rest in being accepted by Him.** In Psalms 46, the writer tells us all about the mighty works and power of God and then instructs us to "be still and know that I am God" (Psalm 46:10 ESV).

Some might say, "Yeah, but I have not been a Christian long enough. I have not done anything significantly good yet. I still have bad habits. I am still tempted. I haven't joined the church yet." I pray that this chapter has shed new light on the powerful truth of being accepted by God. Our wholeness doesn't come from others approving us or liking us. I have good news for you today! Jesus accepts you today, not because of what you have accomplished, but because you put your faith in what He accomplished!

What if the power in Jesus' death and resurrection was more significant than the stench of your old life that still lingers? What if Jesus is so good that no matter how far away you are from your competition or peers, you are accepted by the only one that matters?

Wholeness is about being accepted by God.

CHAPTER NINE

WHOLENESS IS ABOUT BEING A CHILD OF GOD

... for he calls us his children, and that is what we are!

—1 John 3:1 NLT

Wholeness is about **being** accepted, and the first place this becomes evident is in **being** accepted as a **child**. In chapter 7, we discussed that wholeness is about being, not doing. In this chapter, we will develop that a little further.

Since we all come from different families, we each have a different context for what it is like being in a family. Sometimes our view of family is contaminated because of how broken our particular situation has been. It is challenging for many people to understand how awesome being in God's family is because their only view of family is shadowed. Maybe this is your scenario. Let's open our minds and hearts to the possibility that being a child of God could be the absolute best thing going for us. It could be that good.

When Jesus teaches us how to pray, he begins the prayer with our greeting to God. This beginning is crucial: "Our Father which art in heaven..." (Matthew 6:9 KJV). It would seem appropriate to address the God of the universe as, "Oh, Holy Supreme Being" or, "King of the World". Instead, Jesus leads us in the warmest of greetings. Not only is it "Father", but it is "Our Father" giving it the personal, possessive meaning. God is the believer's personal Father.

If He is our Father, then it makes sense that we are His children.

The Father proclaimed love for His Son, when Jesus was baptized. When Jesus approached the Jordan River that day to experience baptism, no one outside of family and neighbors knew him because he hadn't performed any miracles or preached any sermons. He was basically an unknown carpenter's son from Nazareth. John baptized him in the Jordan River, and, as he appeared from the water, something truly spectacular happened. The skies parted and a voice from heaven proclaimed, "This is my dearly loved Son, who brings me great joy" (Matthew 3:17 NLT).

As I stated in a previous chapter, Jesus was declared the Son of God before he did anything spectacular. Not only is he God's Son, but the voice also makes it known that Jesus brings great pleasure to the Father. Jesus was baptized into this identity as God's Son. Interestingly, even though an audible heavenly voice claimed him as a son, he would continually face the temptation to believe this position with God was not the immutable truth. In fact, the very next chapter, we read of the devil tempting Jesus in the desert with the phrase, "*IF* you are the son of God..." (Matthew 4:3 emphasis mine).

This profound truth of identity is something that we all must confront. Confront may seem like a harsh word, but frankly, we need this truth to be settled deep within us. Most of us have the lie of Satan deeply rooted in our hearts. This lie tells us that we are on our own, that we must strive for our position with God, that we have messed up too much, or that we could never be a part of His Kingdom. Because its roots are so intertwined with our core beliefs of who we are, everything that we do or say comes from that foundation.

We need this whole truth of God to confront our broken view of self. Being in God's family can transform our sense of belonging and connection with God and others. When we see Jesus' status with God in the waters of baptism, it is a prophetic proclamation for all those in the future who will call on His name. We become sons and daughters of God through Jesus.

God as Our Father

I love how the characters of the Bible give us bold declarations of who God is. They express how powerful He is and yet how personally He related to them. David said:

The Lord is King! Let the nations tremble! He sits on his throne between the cherubim. Let the whole earthquake!

The Lord sits in majesty in Jerusalem, exalted above all the nations. Let them praise your great and awesome name. Your name is holy! Mighty King, lover of justice, you have established fairness. You have acted with justice and righteousness throughout Israel. Exalt the Lord our God! Bow low before his feet, for he is holy! (Psalm 99:1–5)

The Apostle Paul gave a clear picture of God in his letter to the Romans: Oh, how great are God's riches and wisdom and knowledge! How impossible it is for us to understand His decisions and His ways! For who can know the Lord's thoughts? Who knows enough to give Him advice? And who has given him so much that He needs to pay it back? For everything comes from Him and exists by His power and is intended for His glory. All glory to Him forever! Amen. (Romans 11:33–36)

These two passages are samples of the consistent message throughout the Bible. God is spectacular. We cannot wrap our minds around how amazing He truly is, and yet at the same time, He is not an abstract ruler on a throne detached from His subjects. He is our Father.

He is a father who issues pure love. He has never made a mistake. He knows everything that could be known. God is the creator of the world. He spoke a word, and the light shined. All of the Universe, from the galaxies down to single atoms, comes from the mind of God. God lives outside of our dimension of time and is unbound by the limits of space. And He is our Father.

But I do not deserve to be His kid...

Many have heard this concept of being God's kids for a long time. We know all about it in our heads, but the truth of it is not solid in our hearts. The main reason for this is because of our rebellion. We struggle to accept that God loves us and welcomes us home because we know how broken we are. Our human mind struggles with reconciling our sin with God's amazing love for us. How could this all work together? Jesus gives us the perfect story in the Bible to illustrate this divine work.

There was a very prosperous father who had two sons. The father loved each son. The younger one was interested in getting out on his own and desired a head start. He asked his dad if he could take his inheritance early and use it as an investment in his future. It seemed like a good idea since all young people need help going on their way. It was not long after he launched into his journey that the young son's appetite for pleasure started getting out of hand, and his ability to wisely use his inheritance fell apart. The young man spiraled out of control and ultimately lost all of his money. He was unable to live any decent lifestyle. Matters worsened when the economy turned south and a job was hard to come by. Finally, he persuaded a farmer to hire him, and he worked feeding the farmer's herd of pigs. He became so destitute and hungry that the pig's food looked appealing to him.

It dawned on the young man that even his father's servants lived a better life than he did. The young man started devising a plan to return home, plead his case, and be allowed in as a servant. He knew that returning as a son was too much to ask. However, it was possible that being a servant would be acceptable to his father, and he would live the rest of his life with some stability. He began his journey home with embarrassment. Along the way, he rehearsed the speech he would give his father. He needed to get it just right. If everything went well, he would be accepted back on the property and allowed into the servants' quarters.

Little did the son know that his father's love far transcended anything he could imagine. As he neared the family farm, his heart pounded harder with each step. On the day of his arrival, his father happened to be outside and could see a traveler drawing closer down the road. As he drew closer, his father recognized his long-lost son walking home. He immediately began to run toward his son! The father's greeting was overwhelming—an outpouring of ecstatic love and joy for the sight of his prodigal son.

The son pulled himself away from his father's hug and immediately pleaded his case for returning home. His father eagerly welcomed him back to the family. The son remorsefully petitioned for a spot as a servant. The scene goes like this in the book of Luke:

'Father, I have sinned against both heaven and you, and I am no longer worthy of being called your son.' But his father said to the servants, 'Quick! Bring the finest robe in the house and put it on him. Get a ring for his finger and sandals for his feet. And kill the calf we have been fattening. We must celebrate with a feast, for this son of mine was dead and has now returned to life. He was lost, but now he is found.' So the party began. (Luke 15:21–24)

His father was not paying attention to the son's plea because he was preoccupied with planning the welcome home celebration. The father called out for some essential items not only for the party but for identity. The meal would be the most tender, choicest cut of meat on the farm. The son's clothes were in awful condition and smelly. The father ordered him to be cleaned and clothed with the finest robe. The other two items had enormous significance. The sandals signified that he was a free man. On his hand, a ring was placed, probably a signet ring, which would give him the authority of his father. Rings were worn as a sign of authority and authenticity. They gave the wearer the ability to sign or agree to covenants in the family name (Hendricksen, 756).

What did the son do to deserve this type of treatment? Nothing. What did the son say to convince his father that he was worthy of a second chance? Nothing. Returning home was the only thing the father wanted. The son's plea was not necessary to earn the father's forgiveness or to receive restoration to the family.

The prodigal son found wholeness when he started walking down the road to dad's house. The son found wholeness before he changed clothes or took a bath. He found wholeness before he put on the robe or the ring. The father's declaration of sonship over the young man completely changed him from being the prodigal to being his son.

All of humanity is like the prodigal son. Although we were created by God with great intentions for our lives, we have squandered almost every opportunity. We sit in our current status with no real claim to being a son or daughter. There is nothing we can do to prove ourselves worthy of our sonship. Many of us think that maybe we could go back to God and beg for forgiveness. We hope that He will extend a little grace and we can squeak into heaven. Others cannot imagine God ever offering that, so they do not even try.

Our problem is that we try to understand God's love and forgiveness through the lens of human love and forgiveness! Looking through that lens, forgiving and forgetting seems impossible. The reality is that God's love and forgiveness far exceed our imagination. The truth is, if any of us walks (like the prodigal) down the driveway to God, He will welcome us back into our sonship without hesitation and unconditionally. The love of God transcends the ugliest parts of our life. His goodness outrivals Satan's best efforts.

When I see my relationship with my three kids, I begin to see a new side of God's love for me as a son. In essence, I see my life represented by my kids. Let me explain. My two sons are funny, athletic, good looking, and talented. I could go on and on about how awesome they are. My heart beats so strongly for both of them. I love to watch them play sports, learn in school, talk to girls, and hang out with each other. At the same time, they mess up, fight with each other, and cause their mom and me some stress.

Kennady has never said a word to me. Some days she smiles and laughs at me, and other days, she zones out and doesn't express any emotion. She is unable to read, write, walk, talk, explain, or produce. She hugs better than anyone on the planet and, at the same time, takes more attention and work than anyone else I know.

Here is the truth, at the end of every day, I love all three of my kids exactly the same. Whether they are nailing it as winners or unable to accomplish anything, my love for them does not change. They do not earn the right to be my kids by the way they perform. They are Steeles. They are my kids. They get all the rights and privileges that come with being my kids. Those privileges include affection, teaching, correction, and recreation. In the same way, our Father in heaven loves each of us equally. Our performance on Tuesday or Saturday does not change who we are or our place of belonging.

I pray that my love for my kids mimics God's love for me. I want to be a picture of His love for my kids. However, at some point, my love for them will not be enough to make them into who they need to be. My love cannot save them from themselves. They will need to receive and understand the love of God to transcend them to their heavenly identity as children of God.

When it comes to our identity as children of God, we are released from striving. Striving does not get us into the family, and it does not keep us in the family. However, it seems so difficult to live in that peace because most of us have lived for decades separated from that truth. We either did not know God at all, or we were so preoccupied with gaining His favor that we squandered the peace that could have been ours. You do not have to accomplish something in the next thirty years to make a name for yourself. Living in the family of God is about leaning into God's love and not longing for God's love. You already have a good name. You are in the best family ever. Think about resting in the Kingdom as if you have already arrived.

Our life's meaning and wholeness begin with simply being a child of God.

| CHAPTER TEN | WHOLENESS IS ABOUT BEING COMFORTABLE WITH GOD'S PLAN |

When I lose control, control is not lost.

—Dr. Jeffrey Garner

Two days after Kennady was born, Erica and I had one of the most important conversations of our life. Erica was still admitted as a patient in the hospital because of her C-Section recovery. I had just spent some time with Kennady in the Neonatal Intensive Care Unit. She was hooked up to multiple tubes with nurses attending to her every need. The thought of taking care of a special needs child for the rest of my life crushed me emotionally. At the same time, I wanted the best for my daughter. I could not stand the thought of her physically suffering or going through social rejection. I was coming to the conclusion that I was completely out of control. Nothing I did would change the outcome.

As I walked into Erica's hospital room, we started

talking about our life, our marriage, and our daughter. We talked about the current condition as well as the future of our young family. It felt like we were at a dead-end. How could this scenario possibly work? How could we continue to be Christ-followers and live in this grueling situation?

I finally concluded what I thought was quite profound. After considering all the options and potential outcomes, I told Erica, "I pray that one of two things happen. First, I pray that God completely heals Kennady from head to toe, and she is able to function as a normal girl." I believed (and still do) that God was able to heal every cell in her body and make every function and system work together in perfect synchronicity. I desired for God to make this situation right by restoring her body and making it physically and mentally right.

Then, I added my plan B, "If He chooses not to heal her, I pray that He will simply take her home and that she will be able to dance on streets of gold in heaven with total freedom." With this second prayer, I had come a long way. Usually, death is something that we fight and think is the worst-case scenario. However, I could not conceive of a whole life in her currently disabled state. I was finally accepting that death might be the best option for our daughter. In my mind, there were only two plausible solutions for Kennady.

At the time, I thought that plan B was a huge step. It was. When you get to the point where you accept death as a worthwhile option for your kid, you have come a long way from the moments of dreaming and planning for their future. This was a big step in our faith journey—a place where we were trusting God for more than what we could understand. We put our desires on the back burner and began to trust God for an outcome that would be, ultimately, the opposite of the dreams we held for our young family.

Plan A went into action first. We prayed fervently for Kennady's healing. We organized teams, sent emails, and placed phone calls to people all over the world. We feel blessed to be connected to prayer warriors all over America, Mexico, Brazil, England, Germany, Israel, Nigeria, Romania, India, Zimbabwe, and many places in between. Giants in the faith, including pastors, evangelists, and people who operated in the gifts of healing and miracles, surrounded us in prayer.

For years we prayed for Kennady to talk, walk, eat, learn, and be a normal person until, finally, I became exhausted. I realized that I spent so much time praying for her to be different that I did not value who she was in the moment. Plan A did not happen.

Kennady has brushed with death a few times. Once, when she was 2 years old, she contracted pneumonia and was hospitalized in ICU for eleven days. Erica and I spent those nights in the hospital wondering and praying, "God, what in the world is happening here?" There have been multiple hospital stays, surgeries, and therapies. We have seen dozens of kids across the nation pass away with her same condition. As a pastor, I have done many funerals for children and adults over the last 16 years. Kennady keeps on ticking! Plan B did not happen, either.

God had an unfathomable Plan C for Kennady's life. Instead of being fully healed or passing away, Kennady has lived consistently, day in and day out, as a severely disabled young woman. Kennady wakes up in the morning and patiently waits for someone to come to reposition her or transfer her to the wheelchair. She is unable to roll over, turn on the TV, or even call out for us to help her. Breakfast, lunch, and dinner are a blended liquid. We mix it up each evening and continually fill a bag throughout the day that delivers the food directly to her stomach via a tube. She is unable to use a toilet, so we have to change four to six diapers per day. Kennady suffers from high muscle tone, which means that they continuously flex all day long. Of course, this means fatigue and spasms that can be quite painful. We give her around ten medications per day that control her kidneys, hormones, muscle tone, digestive system, and manage pain. For over eighteen years now, we have bathed her, dressed her, brushed her teeth, and fixed her hair— day in and day out.

At the same time, our family does not feel in any way cheated with Plan C. In fact, the opposite is the case. We feel blessed beyond measure. When we meet people for the first time, (and our kids are not there), God's grace is on display. We look and act like parents of healthy kids. We are not haggard or depressed. We love to laugh and talk about everyday life. There is always a point in conversations with parents where you start talking about your kids, giving details on gender, age, and the like. When we start talking about our three kids, we usually do not speak about Kennady's condition. So, they have no idea about her situation. There is always this fantastic moment when we either tell them later, or when they meet her for the first time, and their mouth drops open. They are stunned because we seemed so "normal," energetic and full of life.

We have an amazing life. We have a ton of friends that we enjoy. We have an amazing church family that not only create a community for us but supports us financially. Our parents live in the area and are a strong foundation for us. Along with our parents, we have caregivers who work with Kennady, which allows us to go on vacations, date nights, grocery shopping, and have a "normal life." All the while, when they are not there, we have to feed, clothe, bathe, and do everything else you can imagine for our 18-year-old daughter.

I think it is vital to express all of these truths because it begins to paint the picture of God's grace in our lives. God supplies a daily allotment of grace to the Steele home measured precisely to what we need to face the challenges and the victories. We never envisioned God would use this plan C to demonstrate His greatness. **Sometimes our unanswered prayers will paint a better picture of**

**God's power and grace than if we would have gotten
what we wanted in the first place.** We package our
logical reasoning with all of our life experience and create
different options for our path. We love being in control of
situations because that typically removes all fear. When
we know that we have a plan A and a plan B, then we are
at ease to approach life. We are not stressed because we
have confidence in our plan. The only problem with this
scenario is that it eliminates God from the picture. It puts
YOU in the position of God. In reality, God has something
unimaginable going on for us. When God is present, we
will never sacrifice peace, contentment, or joy.

As bad as life can be, God is always better. My dear
pastor friend and mentor, John Ragsdale, says it like this,
"When we say that our life is 'not good enough,' God
replies that He is 'God enough.'"

The great prophet, Isaiah said, *"Since the world began,
no ear has heard, and no eye has seen a God like you, who works
for those who wait for Him!"* (Isaiah 64:4)

Then Paul quoted this passage in his letter to the
Corinthians when he said, "No eye has seen, no ear has
heard, and no mind has imagined what God has prepared
for those who love Him." (1 Corinthians 2:9)

So, this brings us to an essential question: Why do
we fight so hard to maintain control of our lives? This
central place of control fundamentally sets our course
and viewpoint for life. Because our entire outlook on

life hinges on who controls it, it begs an answer to the question: Who *is* in control of your life?

Our greatest fear is that if we lose control, then we are simply at the whims of nothingness. While in a discipleship session with Dr. Jeffrey Garner, we dove into this topic, and he said something so simple yet profound. He said, "When we lose control, control is not lost."

As soon as I heard this, peace permeated the atmosphere. God was saying to me, "Robin, when you lose control of your life, that is where I want you and me to be. I want you to lose control so that I can take the reins of your life."

The bigger truth is that God does not want us to wait until we "lose" control as if we had no other choice. He does not wish us to come to the end of ourselves, although many times, that is how it ends up working. The truth is that God wants us to give up control freely. God wants us to let go.

The writer of Hebrews gives us the perfect way to look at this. He is expressing awe and wonder of God's creation of humans and the world. God made us the stewards of this great planet.

The writer of Hebrews gives us the perfect way to look at this. He is expressing awe and wonder of God's creation of humans and the world. God made us the stewards of this great planet.

'You put all things under his control.' For when he put all things under his control, he left nothing outside of his control.

*At present we do not yet see all things under his control, **but we see Jesus**, who was made lower than the angels for a little while, now crowned with glory and honor because he suffered death, so that by God's grace he would experience death on behalf of everyone. (Hebrews 2:8–9 NET)*

I love that phrase in the middle. *"At present, we do not yet see all things under His control, **but we see Jesus**..."* That says it all. Right now, we do not see things the way we want or expect to see them. However, we see Jesus. Maybe it would help us if it read, *Jesus is ready, willing and available for you to look at Him. If we look to Jesus and all He is capable of doing in our lives, then we would not be concerned with things not being under our control right now.*

A couple of years ago, I went on a forty-day sabbatical. For over five weeks, I did nothing related to the church or pastoring. We went on a two-week road trip. I binge-watched the Beverly Hillbillies. I worked on our house. I was bored, and that was the point of the sabbatical—rest. When I returned to work, I was better prepared to face the challenges of ministry. Little did I know that I would be thrown into the fire. Instead of gradually getting back into the swing of things, complications started firing at a blazing speed. We had to prepare an annual leaders' retreat, launch small groups, deal with some rogue church members, and Hurricane Harvey hit and wrecked south Texas. An excellent property came available for our family, so we decided to buy it, sell our house and build a new one. All of this happened in one week.

Not all of these scenarios were bad things, but they were important things that required a ton of my attention. I was busy from daylight to after dark. I went from being bored to being frazzled in just a few days. God was putting me and my sabbatical to the ultimate test. I was given way too many things for me to handle by myself. At first, I was trying to plan, organize, figure out, and execute all of them in a neat and orderly fashion. About halfway in, I realized that I was trying to maintain control, and I was not allowing God to be in control of the situation. There was no way that I could pull off all these items and wrap them up in a cute little bow.

Deep down, below the surface of my life, I was not trusting that God's control was better than mine. I was holding on for dear life and thinking all of these things were my responsibility. In reality, they were in my job description, but the ability to finish was well beyond my capacity. **Freedom unfettered me as I realized that when I lost control, God was not mad at me or disappointed that I had failed Him.** The opposite was the case, when I lost the ability to control all the details of life, I put Him back on the throne.

Wholeness comes to our lives when we abdicate control of our lives to God. We dive into a mysterious world of the unknown. Instead of calling all of the shots, we seek God for direction. Instead of only praying to get what we want, we pray to find out what God wants. In our prayers, we invite His will instead of spending all of our time manipulating Him to accomplish ours. We quest. We ask questions. We listen. We trust.

During that season of life where my work and personal life were crazy, I started canceling plans. I gave responsibility and authority to other people. I quit worrying what people thought of my ability to lead. I started believing that God would work out the season in His way.

Here seems to be the sequence of our control issues:

- We dream big dreams.
- We work really hard to accomplish those dreams.
- We experience some success at the hands of our efforts.
- We experience difficulty (starting to lose control).
- We fight to maintain our pace and control of the situation (stress sets in).
- We manipulate people and God to help us.
- We run out of options, and we become depressed.
- We may find coping mechanisms to numb the pain, ignore the situation, or detach from reality.

In the Bible, we read about a man named Lazarus, who became very ill and died. His sisters reached out to Jesus for help during the sickness because they happened to be close friends with him. They were thinking, *If only Jesus gets here soon, then everything will be ok.* Mary and Martha sent a message to Jesus that was a bit manipulative. "...Lord, your **dear friend**, is very sick" (John 11:3 NLT emphasis mine). They pleaded with Jesus to come to their brother's rescue and added the personal, affectionate "your dear friend," to strengthen the plea. They desperately wanted God to work on their behalf to heal their brother. However, Jesus did not go.

Well, Jesus did go, but he waited two full days before he began his journey to Lazarus' bedside. Jesus was not concerned. He rested in the power of God and knew that not only was healing a possibility, but being raised from the dead was no big deal. Time was not an issue for Jesus. He knew that waiting was probably better for Mary and Martha in the long run. This scenario of God showing up supernaturally for them and Lazarus would reshape the way they viewed God going forward. They would learn that God works on His schedule, that we do not have to dictate the exact parameters of His work, and that often we find ourselves completely helpless. Mary and Martha were out of control, but God was not.

Ultimately, this control issue points us to something about God's nature. God can handle every single life situation in His way and turn it into something amazing because He is truly GREAT. Being great is in His essence; it is who God is, and yet His greatness is something that we are tempted to doubt. The devil has been trying to get us to believe something opposite about God's greatness since the Garden of Eden. The twist and turns of our lives, throw us into scenarios where we are tempted to believe something untrue about God's nature.

Look at how the prophet Isaiah described God's nature compared to ours:

'My thoughts are nothing like your thoughts,' says the Lord. 'And my ways are far beyond anything you could imagine. For just as the heavens are higher than the earth, so my ways are higher than your ways and my thoughts higher than your thoughts.' (Isaiah 55:8–9)

I encourage you to stop reading the book for a few moments and meditate on that passage. Reread it and compare it to the way you are handling life right now.

When Isaiah writes this, it is not merely for his situation or even that particular time. Isaiah prophetically proclaims this message about God's divine nature as it relates to your life in this era. It reads as words coming directly from God's mouth towards us. Failures from our past contaminate our thoughts. Reason, logic, and scientific methods limited by man's experience, mire our thoughts. We stop looking for God's ways because the ways of the world are screaming at us at every turn. Man's way is tweeted, posted, streamed, broadcast, and written about on a second by second basis in our society. We do not have to dig very deep to find the methods and thoughts of people.

At the same time, God's ways are equally available to

those who have an ear to hear. He gives us an analogy to understand His greatness. Just as the heavens are so high and unreachable by the physical world, God's ways are higher and unattainable by us. We cannot even reach or contain God's ways. He is too great. The only way to participate in His ways is to surrender to them. **We have to give up the idea that we will somehow maintain control of our lives and tap into God's resources at the same time.**

Jesus Christ embodies the concept of God's greatness and, at the same time, models how humans are to face a struggle. In this one man, we see the merging of humanity and deity. We find our strength in trusting Jesus Christ because he met all the horrible realities of this world without losing hold on the truth of who God is. Jesus experienced people's fickle loyalty, selfish ambition, and fear of each other. He was abandoned by his closest friends and then given the impossible task of willingly walking to his crucifixion. In the Garden of Gethsemane, when Jesus faced his awaiting death, he talked to God about control. "Is there any other way? Can we do this differently, in a way that might be easier on me? No? Ok, let's do it your way" (Mark 14:36, that's my own translation).

This book opened with Sam's story of living sixty-two years as a deaf man. I asked Sam the profound question, "Sam, is it possible to be a deaf person and a whole person at the same time?"

Are you ready for the answer?

Without missing a beat, he passionately signed, "I strongly believe that God made me as who I am for a reason. I believe that God had a reason for me to be deaf."

Ok, hang on a second! Rewind the clip a little bit. When little Sammy is crawling around on the blanket as a baby, we have a particular vision of how life is supposed to go, and it does not include being deaf. We cannot envision a life without sound as being fulfilling or whole, yet Sam has discovered that wholeness is not predicated on being in control. Wholeness is wholly dependent on surrender. Sam trusts that God is in control and that His control is better than Sam's control. Sam has experienced the empowering Spirit of God fulfilling each of his needs.

Surrender to God's plan and control brings relief. Sam boldly proclaims the value of his life and the comfort that he lives in because of his trust in God's ways. Sam is whole not because he can function with all of his sense, but because he is resting in God's greatness. A great place for us all.

What is God preparing right now for your life? What is your plan C?

PART THREE

How to LIVE Whole

CHAPTER ELEVEN | TALKING TO GOD

Prayer is a personal, communicative response to the knowledge of God.

—Timothy Keller

Regularly talking to God is the only way to rest in your wholeness. The churchy word for these conversations is prayer, but do not get distracted or intimidated by that word. God wants to talk to you.

Recently, someone asked me how our prayers have changed since Kennady has come into our lives. My answer? "Entirely." The only way that we have been able to cope with suffering is to surrender to God's plan in prayer. The only way we have been empowered to live victoriously is to be filled with the sweet presence of the Holy Spirit. Without prayer, we find ourselves focusing on the work, the question marks, and the uncertainty. Without prayer, we default to logic to solve problems.

When I say "we," I'm not ambiguously talking about humans in general. I am talking about Erica and me. We are always tempted to live like this is all up to us. Our conversations with God remind us of who we are, who God is, and how we are to relate to each other.

Remembering who God is and who we are is the most important part of any prayer. Prayer's goal is to take us deep below the surface of our lives, from where our identity and priorities come. We get so distracted with our interactions at home, work, school, and elsewhere that we start centering ourselves on almost anything except God. An authentic conversation with God will reinforce and refresh the foundation of our wholeness. God accepts us, we are God's kids, and God is in control. When we talk to God the way Jesus teaches us, we cannot remain in a state of self-centeredness. Prayer reminds us that God has already finished the work of earning our place with Him in Jesus. These conversations with God keep us this in place of peace.

WHAT IF WE ARE NOT GOOD AT PRAYER?

Communication is so difficult for me. You would think, as a pastor, that I would like talking to people or that I would be good at it. Unfortunately, neither is the case. I was born with some natural gifts, but talking to people is not one of them. I am a loner at heart and love doing things by myself. I love going to restaurants by myself, going to movies by myself, even watching the Super Bowl by myself. Weird, huh? So when it comes to talking to others one-on-one, I clam up.

During those brutal teenage years, I actually wrote a cheat sheet before calling girls on the phone. I racked my brain trying to think of interesting things to say and then actually write down a list in a strategic order. I was determined to sound like a cool guy that flowed naturally in conversation. I dreaded the idea of having to think on the fly; with my handy cheat sheet I could keep things flowing along. Laugh if you will, but it worked!

I can recall a time when our church was still new, and my skills were put to the test. The mayor of San Marcos invited me to a mixer at the president of Texas State University's house. All the prominent leaders of our town would be in attendance. We were to meet the candidates for city manager and then give the mayor feedback on what we thought. Mixers can be very challenging in that there are no planned activities other than...talking to each other! We had to walk around the room eating Triscuits and ranch dip, acting like we all wanted to be there. I needed my cheat sheet! Somehow, I stumbled through it, met a few new people, and survived the night.

For years, I tripped through conversations with God in the same way. I was taught how to pray; I had examples to follow, role models for it in my life, terrific parents and pastors. Most of my friends were Christians, also. I went to church every week and said "grace" over every meal.

However, while growing up, I struggled to find my own voice with God. In moments of desperate need, I offered up fervent pleas to God. When times were especially good, I offer up quick thanks. However, these moments did not feel like the exchange of ideas with two parties who were intimately connected. Instead, they seemed very ritualistic and rehearsed.

For any conversation to be connected and meaningful, there needs to be good rhythm, rapport, and consistency. Each party in a conversation needs to participate. There has to be talking and listening. Earlier in my walk with God, I struggled in those three areas. I was doing all the talking with God (no rhythm). I did not have a firm grip on what I meant to God and who He was to me (weak rapport). Each session seemed to be sporadic, depending on my particular mood (poor consistency).

Sadly, talking to God is complicated and intimidating for most people. Let's change that! I love the Timothy Keller quote posted at the beginning of this chapter from his book, *Prayer*: "Prayer is a personal, communicative response to the knowledge of God." Most people struggle talking to God and feel bad for not doing it. They strive to be motivated and interested. They want more tools to know how to converse with God. What Keller says in this powerful statement is that authentic conversations with God are responses to our knowledge of who God is. In other words, if there is a problem with our discussions with God, then it goes back to a root problem of not knowing who God is. A healthy core knowledge of God creates the motivation and passion for God-filled conversations. If God approves of us, we are His kids, and He is in total control of all situations, then it makes perfect sense for us to talk to Him on a regular basis.

When we scan the Bible for solid examples of people who knew how to talk to God, one sticks out above the crowd—Daniel. Daniel lived and worked in a high-stress environment. He had been taken from his homeland, stripped of his family and friends, and thrown into a pagan society. The Babylonians were not just liberal in their theology and ways; they opposed Israel's way of life. In America, we often struggle with people who have different political views, and we refer to that as persecution. The Babylonians force Daniel and his friends into a completely new way of life. They were in a different sphere when it came to religion, home-life, occupation, and even food.

After the Babylonians took control of Israel, many of the Jews were sent to live in Babylonia. Daniel and two other young men were among the Jews captured. The king selected these three men from the group of Jews and thrust them into his special forces. These young men were to rigorously train, study, and prepare for the king's service. The king stripped from them everything that had given them their identity. They were foreigners in every sense of the word.

You might say that Daniel and his friends were

not living the life that they had probably imagined for themselves. They were living out a "plan C." The characteristics of their work life, social life, and religious life were not transpiring as planned. Instead of carrying on the traditions of Israel in Judea, they were learning the culture of heathens. Daniel faced the challenge of living in foreign surroundings while at the same time, holding on to his lifelong beliefs about God. The only way that Daniel made it was by talking to God.

Amid all the opposition and distraction, Daniel excelled through the ranks and became one of the king's most influential men. The king had plans for Daniel to be in charge of the entire kingdom. When word got out that Daniel had found such favor with the king, other Babylonians became extraordinarily jealous and conspired to remove Daniel from such a prominent role, eventually having him thrown into a lions' den. It is in the context of this pressure cooker that we get a glimpse of Daniel's conversations with God.

In this hostile situation, Daniel conversed with Jehovah daily. His relationship with God and his lifestyle that nurtured it teach us a valuable lesson. When our desire to talk with God is real and authentic, persecution and death cannot deter us.

Many of us allow life to deter us from talking to God; the football game is on, we need to get to work early today, or we need to take the kids to soccer practice. Our passion and intent to talk with God is thwarted by menial tasks and everyday activities—not a lions' den! Our first temptation is to read Daniel's story and consider that our solution may be to create a spiritual discipline. So we think, *I need to pray, and I want to be like Daniel. So I will choose three times during my day to stop and pray.* We even set alerts on our phone, displaying our sincere intentionality.

The first time the alert goes off, we are excited about it. "Yeah! I want to be like Daniel," we say. We drop what we are doing and begin thinking about God. Then, later in the day, it happens again. Feeling good about ourselves, we think, *Wow! I am really like Daniel now.*

After a couple of days, we find we've had to cancel a few times, and, within a week, we have wholly abandoned the system. Now our thoughts shift to a guilty stream whenever it crosses our minds. *I'm not like Daniel. I have failed God. I couldn't even keep it up for one week!*

I cannot tell you how many times I played that type of situation out with different spiritual disciplines throughout my life. I always felt like I was not strong enough and that I was a bad Christian. I was not good at it. When bad things happened in my life, I would think, *It is because I am not good at being a Christian, if I could simply talk to God more and be more focused on doing these Christian activities, then I would have a different outcome.*

Things finally changed for me when I realized my main problem was not a discipline problem. My main problem was that I did not have a true understanding of who God was and who I was in relation to Him. As

Timothy Keller said, "I did not have true knowledge of God and therefore, I had no consistent or meaningful response to dialog with Him." If we try to develop spiritual disciplines and religious procedures without first starting with the proper knowledge of God, then we are setting ourselves up for failure. Daniel spoke to God three times a day because he knew God intimately. It would have been impossible for him to maintain any religious habit amid a Babylonian world unless that habit grew out of a deeply rooted, authentic relationship with God.

Please hear me out. I am not talking about an emotional, salvation experience. Many people have a passionate moment with God when they first come to place their faith in Him. This is a powerful, legitimate moment with profound meaning. However, it is our first encounter with God. We cannot expect to know Him at this point. We hear about God and His good news. We experience Him, and our soul finds freedom. We begin to place our faith in Him for salvation. However, at this point, we are far from a deep relationship with Him. We cannot expect to have enough relationship equity with Him at this point for rich, consistent conversations. **It is when we are resting in our position with God that our conversations with Him go deep.**

We should not expect our conversations to be as consistent or thorough with God until we know Him better. Think about it this way: **Our attention span is longer the more we LIKE someone.**

There could be someone talking to you with all the knowledge in the world. However, they could be so dull, arrogant, or verbose that no matter how much they articulate or pontificate, you do not want to talk to them because of what you know about them.

The opposite is true as well. We love our kids. When our kids are too young to be understood, we will listen intently to their babbling, straining to pick out words that we recognize. We are intently listening. We are eager to communicate with our kids. Those of you who don't have kids, have dogs. You talk to and listen to your dogs. YOU KNOW YOU DO! We do this because we love them and know them.

Moms and dads never change. I love hearing my 13 and 15 year old speak to me. I sit beside my daughter, who is 18 and unable to form words, and yet I work eagerly to decipher her nonverbal communication. (She loves me more than Momma.) I love to hear from my kids! Why? Because I know them deeply. I understand who they are to me and who I am to them.

My mom and dad love to get calls from their 43-year-old son (me). About what? Nothing. They would like to talk about nothing. What do they want to hear from me? Anything. Call me. Let's talk They desire to speak with me, not because of what I can offer them or what interesting info there is to share. In an intimate relationship, the desire to talk is solely based on the value of the relationship. *I want to talk to you because you are you*, is the desire expressed inside us toward those we know and love.

If you struggle in your talks with God, then I encourage you to reread, study, and contemplate the content in chapters 8, 9, 10. Those chapters give clear direction about who God is for you right now! If those truths of BEING whole in God, being God's kid, being accepted by God, and being ok with God's plan for your life are not fully resting in your heart, then you will always struggle in your conversations with God. The conversations we have with God directly relate to our perception of who He is and His thoughts toward us.

HOW DO WE TALK TO GOD?

Most of us have a problem talking to God because **we don't understand how much God likes us.** We don't know how much God is excited about our lives and eager to connect. Our problem as humans is that we judge how much God likes us by how much other people like us or by how much we love ourselves. Therefore, our relationship with God is handcuffed by our mentality and the limitations we put on God.

The very first step in engaging with God is to focus on **WHO you are talking to, NOT on what to say.** Jesus shows us that we are not addressing the king or the president. We are not saluting a boss or taskmaster.

We are talking to our Father. This wording is crucial to understanding our position and role.

Job is an excellent example of someone who went through a journey to learn more about who God is. His mission was brutally hard. As you read the book of Job, you see his prayers change. His journey changed his knowledge of God and thus changed the way he talked to God. At first, he is processing his pain and suffering through prayer, then God reveals Himself to Job. From that point, Job talks to God in repentance and adoration. The more clearly Job saw who God was, the fuller his prayers became—moving from mere complaint to confession, appeal, and praise.

The secret to conversing with God lies not in effort or technique, but our knowledge of God. The more you get to know God as your Father, the longer your attention span will grow for Him. As your attention span grows, you will long for more conversations and they will naturally increase in frequency too. Instead of improving your dialog with God by finding new techniques and systems, make your prayers healthy and inspired by getting to know Him more.

It would be so awesome if we could hear from God and have Him explain Himself to us. Then we would have a clear understanding of who He is. God spoke to Job "out of a whirlwind" (Job 38:1). Oh, how we long for God to show himself to us clearly and distinctly. The truth is that God speaks to us much more clearly than a whirlwind.

Long ago, at many times and in many ways, God spoke to our forefathers through the prophets, but in these last days, **He has spoken to us by his Son***, whom He appointed the heir of all things, through whom also He created the world. He is the radiance of the glory of God and the exact imprint of His nature, and He upholds the universe by the word of His power. After making purification for sins, He sat down at the right hand of the Majesty on high, having become as much superior to angels as the name He has inherited is more excellent than theirs.* (Hebrews 1:1–4 ESV, emphasis mine)

When we get to know Jesus, we know God fully. When we look to Jesus Christ, we are looking at the glory of God through the filter of human nature. When we get to know Jesus, our conversations with God become passionate. Let's get to know God! The easiest way to get to know God is to read the Bible. I will go into this particular idea in the next chapter, but for those who cannot wait, here is a sample: If you are new in your relationship with God, read about Jesus in Matthew, Mark, Luke, and John. Once you read about God in the flesh, you will start to communicate His language little by little.

Most likely, no one reading this book remembers when you learned to speak. Why? Because you were little. Think about the way a small child learns to speak. The child is not trying to learn a language. Instead, that language is being spoken into the child from the parents and others around her.

Eugene Peterson says: We are plunged at birth into a sea of language…then slowly, syllable by syllable, we acquire the capacity to answer: mama, papa, bottle, blanky, no. Not one of these words was a first word….all speech is answering speech. We were all spoken to before we spoke.

Studies have shown that children's ability to understand and communicate is profoundly affected by the number of words and the breadth of vocabulary to which they were exposed to as infants and toddlers (Nicholas 2006). The degree to which we are spoken to, we speak.

When we immerse ourselves in God's Word and presence, we will learn how to pray. It might take as long as it does for a baby to learn his primary language. Do not be concerned if it takes you three or four years before your conversations with God find a healthy rhythm and consistency. To be clear, I am not saying it will take several years before you connect with Him in a meaningful way. We can expect moments with God from the very beginning of our relationship. Through time, our vocabulary will deepen, and our relationship with God will strengthen.

RHYTHMS OF PRAYER

As I have come to know God more closely over the last few years, my own private time with God has changed drastically. I have no more guilt about my prayer life.

Around five times a week (mostly Monday through Friday), I get up early and have around thirty to forty-five minutes of private devotion time with God. My time consists of scripture reading, journaling, and contemplation. Many times, I speak directly to God during these moments, and I hear Him speaking clearly to me. However, there is not a time when I start talking and go for thirty to forty-five minutes straight with me talking out loud. I go with the flow in these moments, and these are the times that I hear from God the most. I also hear from God while jogging. I often go for early morning jogs after my devotion, and I hear so clearly from God during these moments. My mind is a captive audience for God because I cannot do anything else but put one foot in front of the other.

Two times a week, I have a very structured prayer session with two different groups of people. On Tuesday mornings, I gather with my church staff, and we talk to God as a group. We will put on some worship music, or our worship leader will gently play. The first half of the session, we are on our own. We walk around the room, kneel, lay down, and have our private moments with God. We then gather for the remaining time to pray about focused topics. I present a theme, and we all speak to God on that subject. On Wednesday mornings at 6 a.m., the structure is the same, but it is with men from the church. Afterward, we go out for breakfast. We talk a lot. We cry out. We give voice to our thoughts, and we also quote scripture towards God.

As a pastor, I spend several days a week thinking and talking to God about the message I plan to give on Sunday morning. Listening for God's voice throughout the week during my writing and preparation sets the course for the message. Listening to God on Sunday morning before and during the message is huge too.

Also, there are a ton of impromptu conversations with God throughout the week. People come to me with concerns and needs, and I am honored to join with them in talking to God. Jesus teaches us in Matthew 18:20 to always be ready to pray in small groups.

Where I live, in the southern United States, praying for meals is a huge tradition. I know that a lot of Americans and others across the world pray at mealtime, but in the south, people are religious about the pre-meal prayer. In fact, when people forget to pray, others, with a dirty look, will say, "You aren't going to pray for your food?" Or they will say, "You might get food poisoning!" It seems like if we do not pray for our food, we do not love God or that we will die from food poisoning. Several years back, I made a decision My primary intention for the pre-meal prayer is not going to be about food poisoning, and I will not do it out of guilt.

Instead, I will take thirty seconds to stop and remember WHO God is and WHO I am in Him. This perspective has made the moment so much more meaningful for our family.

Spend some time thinking about your current conversations with God and why you participate in them. Find out where and why you struggle. Rest assured that God is ready to speak with you. I believe that He is already speaking to you. Be excited and inspired that as you become whole in God, your talks with Him will be stronger and stronger.

Look forward to the day that you and God consistently relate and converse on all the topics and issues of your life.

CHAPTER TWELVE | HEARING FROM GOD

The Holy Scriptures are our letters from home.
—Augustine of Hippo

What if you were whole and did not even know it? What if you were listening to so many outside voices that the truth was hiding underneath the noise? Thousands of messages hurl towards us at breakneck speed. We give an audience to the ones that bring the most immediate attention or demand the quickest response. Unfortunately, many messages are negative. They make us feel like we need to earn more money, lose more weight, prove ourselves one more time, the list goes on and on. All the while, our Father in heaven is going unheard.

God continually says things like, "You are good. You are mine. You are forgiven. You matter. I made you on purpose. I will protect you. I will provide for you. I will fulfill all your needs. You will be satisfied with me." God desired for us to be whole and worked to see it accomplished. Then, He continually proclaims that wholeness over us. Unfortunately, we do not hear His voice, and over time, we drift from being whole to being fragmented.

Erica and I are no different. Over the years, the difficulties of life have shouted to us. With the continual weight of Kennady's care pulling us down, we have had plenty of opportunities to become discouraged. It is easy to get depressed!

We cannot go anywhere without considering how we will take care of Kennady. Taking a family vacation is almost impossible because of travel limitations. For example, there are changing tables for infants and small children in virtually every public space. However, there are no changing tables for 18 year olds. Kennady requires a full handicapped accessible shower and chair. It is easy to give up on a persistent challenge like this; it is easier just to stay home all the time.

If the physical toll was not enough, we also deal with frequent emotional tidal waves. We have family members who make fun of others by using the "r word." Think about that for a second. They have known us for decades. They know all about Kennady, yet, they indirectly insult and devalue her with cheap words. A few years back, a friend told a group of us a "short bus" joke. The butt of the joke was that people with special needs ride on the "short" school bus. When that happened, I stared him in the eyes and said, "You do realize that my daughter rides the short bus?" He apologized profusely, but the damage was done.

These are just a couple of real-world examples that we face in our world with Kennady. These scenarios are not only challenging to suffer through from a practical standpoint, but a continual barrage over the years reinforces a loud message that we are not going to make it. They figuratively say things to us like, "You have no future. You cannot sustain this. You will run out of money. No one understands you. No one has the capacity to be your friend. You need to give up."

As we go through each day, negative messages bombard us. If we listen to them unprepared, we will be swept away on a journey far from home. We will travel from wholeness to a land of bitter, angry, lost, loneliness, and incompleteness. Most people live in this spot separated from the truth of God. As a result, we try to find our way back to peace in any way possible. Humans spend billions of dollars to get our minds off the mess. We try anything we can to distract ourselves, change our surroundings, or buy our way out of it.

The only thing that genuinely leads us home is hearing our Father's voice. I love what Augustine of Hippo said, *"The Holy Scriptures are our letters from home."* The voice of our Father speaks truth amidst the chorus of confusing voices. In my darkest hours, the only thing that has assured my wholeness has been the truth of God's voice.

Hearing His voice and finding ways to center our lifestyle around it preserves the state of our hearts and minds.

When Jesus walked through desert times (literally a desert). He was tempted by the devil to believe that he was not whole. The only thing that Jesus used to combat the voice of the devil was the voice of his Father! Jesus said something amazing about pursing voices of the earth versus the words of his Father: "People do not live by bread alone, but by every word that comes from the mouth of God" (Matthew 4:4 NLT). Basically, Jesus was saying, "Don't rely on what people say around you. Don't even rely on what this world can provide for you (even if you like the taste). Instead, your heavenly Father's words are continuing to come towards you. Live off of those."

This is a beautiful way to live. Jesus was anchored in wholeness because he chose to listen to the truth from his heavenly Father instead of the words and facts shouting at him. You could make a case that Jesus knew the words of God because he was God himself. However, when Jesus addresses the devil, he uses the words of the Hebrew Bible. Word for word, Jesus quotes the Bible when confronted with the option to believe a lie. This example teaches us that God's Word is like a fountain that continually flows; it is relevant and personal. We can both hear it and read it in the Bible. We all know that we can learn a lot from literature. However, few believe that books can literally speak to you in the moment. The Bible offers just that.

The Bible is a place where we hear God's voice clearly.

I think Timothy Keller says it brilliantly in his book on prayer:

Our conversations with God arise out of immersion in the scripture. We should plunge ourselves into the sea of God's language, the Bible. We should listen, study, think, reflect, and ponder the Scriptures until there is an answering response in our hearts and minds. (Keller 2016, 55)

We dig into God's Word, not to have another religious habit or practice in and of itself. Instead, we delve into God's Word to get to know God better. We want to learn who He is. We want to recognize His voice. We want to learn about His character. When we get to know Him better, we build camaraderie, familiarity, and awe. The more we get to know God, the more we admire and honor Him. One of the best ways to further your relationship with God is to read His Word.

We can vividly see the power of God's Word when we look at the varying levels of life in God's creation. Plants have a form of life that enables them to sense moisture and light, but they cannot see objects. Animals have a higher form of life that allows them to see objects, but they cannot know the difference between instinct and cruelty. People have a still higher form of life that empowers them to see right and wrong, love and beauty. However, because of our fallen condition, we are unable to see higher spiritual realities. When the Word of God comes into a person, it moves him or her to an even higher order of life that the Bible calls the "new life"—participation in the divine nature. When that happens, you can see things you never saw before! (Siegenthaler 2007)

WHAT DOES HE SAY?

When we read His Word, we begin to hear God speak of His love for us. We see our brokenness. We hear of our infinite personal value in the eyes of God. All of these great realities that we were once blind to become apparent when we read His Word.

Throughout scripture, God says to us, "You are good. You are accepted. You are mine. You are forgiven. You are valuable. You have meaning. I will protect you. I will provide for you. I will satisfy you. You can trust me. I made you."

When you take the ugly, heavy messages from others and yourself like—*You are fired. You need to lose weight. You won't finish that degree. I don't love you anymore. Why do you keep messing up like that?*—and line them up side by side with what God is actively saying over you, your wholeness is secure.

BREAKING DOWN THE BIBLE

This sounds awesome, right? The Bible is speaking to us! It brings us home to God's purpose and centers us around His meaning for our lives. Another truth is that the Bible is intimidating. It is such a massive book with intimidating, old English language. Most people never read the Bible because they cannot relate to it. I want to break down some of those barriers by showing you how it is laid out and giving you some practical ways to develop a new reading habit.

THE LAYOUT

Before you start digging into the Bible, it is important to know how each section relates to you as a human in the modern era. The Bible is divided into two major parts. The first section is called the Old Testament and covers everything that happened from the beginning of the world to just before Jesus. The Old Testament includes thirty-nine books, each one with God's voice speaking uniquely and differently than the New Testament. The New Testament covers everything from the birth of Jesus to the present day (and beyond). It includes twenty-seven books.

Old Testament

- **The Beginning** (Books: Genesis–Deuteronomy) These books illustrate the earth's beginning, God's original plan, and humans' rebellion. They also show the beginning of God's plan for redemption, His selection of a people to represent Him, and His very detailed plan for them to follow.

  When we read this section, we see that God is

interested in details. He did not make this world haphazardly. When it comes to our lives, He is involved in each moment. We begin to understand how powerful God is and how much He loves people. God's plan for people is, "You will be my people, and I will be your God." With that covenant comes a very high standard for people to follow. We begin to see patterns of God's faithfulness and humans' inability to perform to any standard.

- **History** (Books: Joshua–Esther) This section lays out the history of God's people, the Israelites. We can relate to their struggle, failure, and need for salvation. We do see some bright examples of people living in wholeness in this section. Although they are not perfect, they are obviously close to God in relationship, and it manifests in their worldly successes. Joshua, Deborah, David, Esther, and others live out their faith in God, surrendering their will to His.

  When we read this section, we hear God proclaim His eternal love for people. We hear God clearly say that our limits do not confine Him. We see the continued themes of human failure and God's sovereignty. As you read through the Old Testament, you will relate to some characters more than others. It is helpful to hang out in those sections. Reread. Pray about those stories and ask

God what He is proclaiming to you. Write down the thoughts you have. Ask others to read and pray with you about what God might be telling you.

- **Poetic** (Books: Job–Song of Solomon) This section is filled with songs and prayers by characters in every phase of life. This is a great place to see how people cry out to God in celebration and disappointment. The Bible does not hide scenarios where people suffer. This is wonderful because it is relatable to us now and shows us how to walk through valleys of life.

  When we read the poetic books of the Old Testament, we learn that the current situation we are facing is not the final word. We learn a vocabulary of praise and worship towards God. We learn that transparency with God is ok. We do not have to pretend like life is easy or enjoyable. God is speaking even in the darkest parts of life.

- **Prophets** (Books: Isaiah–Malachi) This final section of the Old Testament is quite long and difficult to understand for the rookie Bible reader. However, please do not avoid it. This portion of the Bible lays out some of the most explicit messages from God to people. This section recounts God speaking to His people about specific things they are going through at that moment. We also see Him talk about things that have not happened as of the publishing of this book! It covers a lot of ground.

New Testament

- **Gospels** (Books: Matthew–John) Jesus finally arrives on the scene! These four books give eyewitness accounts of Jesus' life on earth. They cover His birth, life, miracles, teachings, death, burial, and resurrection. This section is a favorite for many people. It is straightforward reading and has practical lessons that are ready to be put to use.

  When we read this section, we can hear God speaking to us about our lives. God declares His love toward us in sending us Jesus. We hear of Jesus' purpose, forgiveness, and idea of the Kingdom through each of his stories. If we do not read the Gospels, we will wander forever.

- **History** (Acts of the Apostles)

  Acts is is one powerful, action-packed book. Seriously, this book could stand alone as incredible prose. It tracks the disciples as they begin to live life without Jesus being physically present with them.

  It gives us a model for community relations, faithful praying, and living out our faith on an everyday basis. This book shows how the church grew throughout the first century.

When we read Acts, we can learn how powerful God is and how we can participate with Him to change the world around us. We hear God telling us that He wants us to be a part of this reconciliation with the world.

- **Letters** (Romans–Jude)

  The Apostles write these letters to the first churches of Christianity. I believe one of its key writers, the Apostle Paul, could summarize this section in one word: meat. These letters feed us thick answers to questions we all ask, solutions to things like how we are to walk out our faith, worship God as a community, and reach out to those who are on the outside.

- **Revelation**

  This final book of the New Testament gives us prophetic messages from God. John, the writer, uses a lot of allegory and images to paint the picture of how God's renewal of the world will finally play out.

  When we read this book, we hear God saying that He is still in control. He proclaims His faithfulness to His plan and that His love for us is not in jeopardy. If we do not read this book, we can drown or be lost in the struggle of our moment and forget that the current condition of the world and our reality is not forever. The renewal that began at Jesus' cross will culminate one day in a final victory. Revelation offers an eternal perspective that gives us hope while we live out today.

OPTIONS ON HOW TO GET STARTED

If reading the Bible is new to you or you have struggled in the past to find consistency with reading the Bible, here are some helpful ways to build momentum.

- **Start with the Gospels**

    Instead of starting at the beginning of the Bible, begin where the story of Jesus starts. In particular, the book of John is a great starting point. You will quickly get into the action and into the powerful story of Jesus.

- **Read the book of Acts**

    After reading the Gospels, dig into the book of Acts, which is a historical book that outlines how the first church began. It is filled with adventure and the power of the Holy Spirit.

- **Read from Genesis**

    After you have a grasp on Jesus' life and how the church started, go back and start from the beginning. Genesis teaches how the world started and how the first humans came to know God. You will see just how broken people become without God and how much God pursues broken people.

- **Get a Daily Reading Plan**

    There are a ton of daily plans out there to pace

your reading each day. You can buy Bibles that are divided into daily reading plans. These plans are especially helpful if you have a goal to read the whole Bible in one year.

- **Read Slowly**

  Reading the whole Bible in one year is great to do at least once. However, please don't try to do that every year. Take some time with the scripture. Read one chapter a day, or go even slower. Allow the Word to speak to you. If you do not understand something, then go back over it.

- **Journal**

  Have a notepad and pen ready. Jot down questions. Write down thoughts that come to you. Write out prayers that connect with the scripture you just read. These will be helpful for years to come. It is always a treasure to look back on prayer and scriptural thoughts from previous seasons and see how God has brought you through.

- **Read with Someone**

  Find a small group or a friend that can read the same passages per week and then discuss. Some people like to read a passage each day and then use online forums or email to engage in a discussion on the reading.

- **Read Different Versions of the Bible**

  In this book, I have primarily used the New Living Translation and the English Standard Version. These are written in language that is very easy to understand. It is helpful to read others, such as the New King James Version, and compare how they differ. Sometimes a verse really pops out in different wording.

- **Take a Bible Course Online**

  There are tons of Bible courses online. Find one that has reliable reviews and try it out. It is valuable to have other people's thoughts on the Word.

- **Take Notes in Church**

  This is huge! You have your own private Bible teacher and coach in your pastor. Use him or her to learn more about God's Word. Take notes during the sermon. Go back and read the text during the week. Email questions to your pastor and dig even deeper into the topic!

Friends may be positive; coworkers are encouraging; you can even tell yourself how valuable you are. However, there is nothing like the words of your heavenly Father to bring you home to wholeness. Try a few of these methods and allow God's Word to take root in your soul. His words bring life like nothing else. May the cry of our heart be like the words of this powerful chorus:

Word of God speak
Would You pour down like rain
Washing my eyes to see
Your majesty
To be still and know
That You're in this place
Please let me stay and rest
In Your holiness
Word of God speak
"Word of God Speak"
—*Bart Millard and Pete Kipley*

CHAPTER THIRTEEN | LET'S GET TOGETHER

*But the Christians pressed on, in the conviction that they were a "**colony of heaven**," called to obey God rather than man.*
— Dr. Martin Luther King Jr.

Remember what your mom used to say? "You are who you hang out with. If you hang out with losers, you will be a loser; if you hang out with winners, you will be a winner." I am not sure if your mom said it just like that, but we have all heard advice like that somewhere along the way. Social groups have a strong impact on those who are a part of them. Throughout our lives, we often drift in and out of different groups, and as a result, our personalities, experiences, ideologies, theologies, and all the other "ologies" are influenced by these different subsets of people.

Since the beginning of time, people have congregated and lived in groups. Each group of people have distinct aspects of their lives that we collectively call their culture. These people live together, work together, and have fun together. People in groups talk intimately with each other, exchange thoughts and ideas, create art, and even procreate to add members to the community. When you were born, you were born into a community of people. At some point in your life, usually as you enter adulthood, you have to make conscious decisions about whether you will stay around these people or find a new group of people to connect with.

There are many communities that are informal. There are no initiation ceremonies, no fees, no particular geographic boundaries, or no requirements to join. There are some communities where you do not even realize you are a part of them until several months or years into it. They naturally form because people met at college, a neighborhood, or bar and started hanging out.

In chapter 6, I referenced the crippled man who spent thirty-eight years laying at the community pool. The Bible clearly states that this pool was surrounded with other crippled folks who longed for healing. There were "a multitude of invalids—blind, lame, and paralyzed"—who all congregated around the pool (John 5:3). They were there all day, every day. Here is another very important fact that describes this community of people: When Jesus asks the man, "Do you want to be made whole?" the man explains that he continually tries to get in the water, but no one will help him into it. Others would actually push their way in front of him, blocking him from enjoying the healing waters (John 5:7). Can you imagine how awful this community must have been? People trying to get ahead in life while others are disregarding them and pushing ahead. Sound familiar? #America #21stcentury

This community of people were known for being invalids. Think about that word: invalids. When researching this story and digging into the vocabulary, I made a discovery that I have never realized. The term invalid is used to describe people who are paralyzed and unable to care for themselves. We use the exact same word (pronounced differently) to describe something that is no longer valid. The culture of this community was that they were not valid people. They were physically and spiritually broken. They cared only for themselves. There was a selfish, bitter, and competitive culture prevalent at the pool community.

Something vitally important happens at this point in the story. After meeting Jesus and being made whole, he leaves the pool community for a completely brand-new identity in Jesus. His transformation of body, soul, and spirit means that he no longer fits in at the Bethesda pool community. He is no longer bitter. He is no longer broken. He is no longer in competition with his neighbor. He does not fit in with the old crowd. His new nature means that he belongs with a new group of people.

The Good News of Jesus Christ transforming you and making you whole from the inside out means that you will not fit into the broken, bitter, and confused culture of your old community. Instead, God is now calling you to be a part of a vibrant group of believers who are all walking in the same direction towards Christ. God offers us community as a valuable resource for us to grow in as we continue to live our lives on earth after we have received salvation. In this community, we garner strength from other humans, and we offer our skills, resources, and experience for them to glean from as well.

When the first people received the Good News of Jesus Christ and were saved, the Bible says they devoted themselves to four things. "All the believers devoted themselves to the apostles' teaching, and to fellowship, and to sharing in meals (including the Lord's Supper), and to prayer." (Acts 2:42)

We should take their lead and devote ourselves to those four things:

- The apostles' teaching—the Bible (covered in chapter 12)
- Fellowship (covered in this chapter)
- Sharing meals (covered in this chapter)
- Prayer (covered in chapter 11)

Maybe the strongest word in this passage is not apostles, fellowship, prayer, or any other word but: DEVOTED. Devote is a verb that completely sets the tone for all the other words in the sentence. The new believers devoted themselves to these four primary activities. Devote is such a strong word. Our English dictionaries says that it means: Resolute. Dutifully firm. Unwavering. "To give over or direct (time, money, effort, etc.) to a cause, enterprise, or activity" (Merriam-Webster).

Here is a great example of devotion:

An old man lived alone in Tasmania. He wanted to dig his potato garden, but it was very hard work. His only son, Jesse, who used to help him, was in prison. The old man wrote a letter to his son and described his predicament.

"Dear Jesse, I am feeling pretty bad because it looks like I won't be able to plant my potato garden this year; I'm just getting too old to be digging up a garden plot. If you were here, all my troubles would be over. I know you would dig the plot for me.
—Love, Dad"

A few days later he received a letter from his son.

"Dear Dad, for heaven's sake, don't dig up that garden. That's where I buried the BODIES.
—Love, Jesse"

At 4 a.m. the next morning, the federal police and local police showed up and dug up the entire area without finding any bodies. They apologized to the old man and left. The same day the old man received another letter from his son.

"Dear Dad, go ahead and plant the potatoes now. It's the best I could do under the circumstances.

—Love Jesse" (Source unknown)

Ok, that is not a true story but a very funny example of devotion. When we are devoted to someone, we will go to any lengths necessary to make sure that person is provided for and protected. When we are devoted to something, we will make sure that nothing gets in the way of our connection to it. Hurdles are jumped. Excuses are eliminated. Prices are paid. Question marks are replaced with exclamation marks. Why? Because we are devoted!

Dr. Martin Luther King Jr wrote about this in *Letter from Birmingham Jail* in April 1963:

There was a time when the church was very powerful—in the time when the early Christians rejoiced at being deemed worthy to suffer for what they believed. In those days the church was not merely a thermometer that recorded the ideas and principles of popular opinion; it was a thermostat that transformed the mores of society.

Whenever the early Christians entered a town, the people in power became disturbed and immediately sought to convict the Christians for being "disturbers of the peace" and "outside agitators." But the Christians pressed on, in the conviction that they were "**a colony of heaven**," called to obey God rather than man. Small in number, they were big in commitment. They were too God-intoxicated to be "astronomically intimidated." By their effort and example they brought an end to such ancient evils as infanticide and gladiatorial contests.

Things are different now. So often the contemporary church is a weak, ineffectual voice with an uncertain sound. So often it is an arch-defender of the status quo. Far from being disturbed by the presence of the church, the power structure of the average community is consoled by the church's silent—and often even vocal—sanction of things as they are.

But the judgment of God is upon the church as never before. If today's church does not recapture the sacrificial spirit of the early church, it will lose its authenticity, forfeit the loyalty of millions, and be dismissed.

(King, Letter from Birmingham Jail)

Dr. King beautifully expresses the power and passion of the early church. They faced a tremendous amount of persecution, and instead of disbanding and shirking in fear, they met that trouble with unity. In this letter, he calls them the "colony of heaven." This term has been used for hundreds of years to illustrate the role of the church in the surrounding of darkness.

A "colony of heaven" actually unearths a much deeper

concept about God and the present-day world. When Jesus prayed, he said, "**Thy kingdom come. Thy will be done in earth, as it is in heaven" (Matthew 6:10 KJV).**

Jesus is calling for God's kingdom to be IN earth, as it is IN heaven. He desires for there to be no separation between the two dimensions. Many people think that we must wait to experience heaven until after we die and the end of time comes. However, Jesus presents something much different here. He says that we should pray for that reality to be present with us now! The reality of heaven can be present regardless of what condition the earth is in. It does not matter what circumstances we are in as people, we can live in a state of heaven here on earth. When Dr. King writes this letter, he is saying that the first church found heaven in their colony of believers. Heaven is in the context of the community of believers.

Of course, Dr. King is writing to people in the mid-1960s when there was a hotbed of turmoil, pain and suffering directly related to race relations between African-Americans and whites. Millions of people were suffering from the ugly effects of racism. This letter brings a challenge and a hope. We can have heaven in the middle of racism. We can be a part of the change. Instead of being a church that is splintered, segregated, and impatient, we can be an authentic, unified colony of heaven that has a voice and makes a difference.

I completely agree with Jesus. Jesus' church or "colony of heaven" is the hope for the world. I agree with Dr. King, we are compromising the power of the church by our selfishness and apathy. The current body of Christ has pockets of power throughout the world, but for the most part is extremely lacking in its unity and significance. The primary reason is that we **no longer devote ourselves to fellowship and sharing meals together**. As long as our priority is living our own lives with our immediate family, then we will continue to drift apart and leave so much potential on the periphery.

WHAT IS FELLOWSHIP?

The early disciples devoted themselves to fellowship and sharing meals together. The concept of fellowship is not complicated. I do not need to give you the original Greek word here to reveal some secret definition of fellowship. We all know what it is. Fellowship is hanging out and doing life together. Sharing laughs, meals, stress, losses, raises, ideas, dreams, and all the other life components. Fellowship goes beyond being acquaintances to becoming friends. This bond of friendship goes beyond a secular definition because it includes discipleship and accountability. A better term to describe it would be brother or sister. In fact, this is exactly what happened in the early church. They began to build bonds that transcended blood relations. Fellowship at its ultimate level is *family*.

The people you hang out with are either centering you

around the profound truth of God and what He has done for you, or they are allowing you to be self-centered. In the previous chapter, we looked at the impact of our heavenly Father's voice. In reality, there will be times when we do not listen. We need other human beings pointing us back to the truth. Our community is able to see that we have drifted. They are around us on a daily basis and can see what we have been blinded to. We need others to be honest and speak things that we might not really want to hear.

Community takes time. It gets messy. Growing together is an investment, and it sometimes takes a while to reap a reward. Instead of leaning into old-fashioned relationships with other people and being patient with the slow process, most of us get weary and give up. Sometimes the relationship breaks up, we hurt one another. We often deal with that by shutting down and avoiding the risk. We toughen our skin and resolve to never be betrayed again.

Others try to beat the system. They try to grow in their faith through a process other than community. Let me explain. Our modern culture has benefitted tremendously over the past hundred years from technological advances. The Industrial Revolution transformed the way we produce everything. Now, when we want to produce a product, we assemble all the components in a factory and send them through a system or a conveyor belt and have the product come out finished on the other side. Over time, we have even replaced humans in factories with machines so that the entire production process is done with computers and robots. Prices have gone down; production and profits have soared.

Unfortunately, in our fear of failure with others, many have adopted an assembly line method for community and relationships. Most of us have modeled our churches after Fortune 500 companies and corporations instead of Biblical examples like grapevines and vineyards. We have used the Industrial Revolution model of factories and assembly lines to build churches and produce disciples. Think about all the systems that churches use right now to eliminate waste, streamline processes, and increase revenue. Trust me, I am neck-deep in this conundrum every day. I am personally convicted about how we have sought after shortcuts.

Hear me out here, I am not saying we need to abandon all technology and live off the grid. I am not saying you need to quit your mega-church. I am saying; however, **we need to rededicate ourselves to each other.** We need to reevaluate how we value our relationships with others and prioritize actual face time with others. Being a follower of Jesus and becoming a disciple does not happen in a factory-type setting. Becoming a disciple of Jesus is not even something that happens after you graduate from a class. Being a follower of Jesus is something that grows over time. Growing as a follower of Jesus happens for the rest of your life. Fellowship is the environment where this process of growth and transformation takes place.

Spend some time thinking about what valid excuses you have to not connect with other believers on a regular basis. Some of the big ones are: You do not have time. You are busy with your job. Your kids have too many things going on. Other people are not like you. They do not have same type of job, education, skin color, church history. Maybe you see yourself as inferior to others. If people really got to know you, they would not be impressed. Your house and possessions are not big enough or good enough to have people over. Go ahead and actually make an honest list of valid reasons why you do not fellowship with others.

They first disciples had many of the same excuses that we have now. Humans all over the world have great reasons why they are not connecting to others. That is not the point. We cannot wait until we have no excuses and then connect to others. Rather, when we are DEVOTED to fellowship, we find answers for every excuse! There may not be perfect solutions for every excuse, but we PUSH THROUGH until we find the value on the other side.

I challenge you to DEVOTE yourself to Christian fellowship over the next three months. Make it one of the most important parts of your calendar. Be intentional and plan for it. See what happens.

Here are some Fellowship Devotion Pointers:

- Intentionally make time for it on your actual calendar. Look at your calendar and see how you can connect with others on your current schedule.
- Keep your eyes and ears open for people that you admire spiritually. Ask if you can intentionally learn from and grow with them.
- Look for people who are earlier in their journey than you. Open your life to a couple of them.
- Get to church early and meet people.
- Stay after church and meet people.
- Go out to eat with someone after church.
- Take your kids to whatever your church offers for them. Make it as important as any other activity like youth sports or dance class. Teach your kids about the value of fellowship.
- Know that it will be a little awkward to begin with. You will have to PUSH through the first few conversations.
- Know that you are taking a risk. These people might do you wrong. This might not work.
- Invite people into your schedule. Invite people into your unkempt life, your sweat pants and no make-up life.
- Ask questions. Find out what makes people tick. Ask more questions. Listen without an agenda.

- Find a small group to join.
- Lead a group.

The Bible is clear. God forgives us and cleanses us from our sin when we have a direct, personal relationship with Him. "But if we **confess** our sins **to him**, he is faithful and just to forgive us our sins and to cleanse us from all wickedness." (1 John 1:9 NLT, emphasis mine)

The Bible is also clear about our healing from sin. Our healing from sin, so that we are not bound or enslaved by it, comes from our personal relationships with each other. "**Confess** your sins **to each other** and pray for each other so that you may be healed." (James 5:16, emphasis mine)

This "each other" part happens when we devote ourselves to fellowship. Find a community of believers and go all in so that you can start being a part of heaven on earth!

THINGS TO PONDER

What are you devoted to? Seriously. What people, places and things do you continually invest in with intense effort? What do you keep on doing? What do you show persistence in practicing?

CHAPTER FOURTEEN | ONE DAY AT A TIME

So don't worry about tomorrow...

—Jesus, Matthew 6:34

Erica and I were shell-shocked a few hours after Kennedy's birth. We were reeling in the emotional exhilaration of birth. Seeing a baby exit the womb and enter the world is the most amazing experience I have ever witnessed. It truly is a miracle. Then, soon after her birth and MRI, we received the news from Dr. Wilson that our daughter not only had fluid on the brain, a condition with hope for healthy living, but she also had a dreadfully worse diagnosis. At that moment, we met with a roller coaster of news that continues to this day.

The weight of diagnosis is so heavy! It feels like a final word spoken over your life. Why does news like that seem so difficult? Later, I dissected the news itself in an attempt to understand why it felt like a ton of bricks. Ironically,

I discovered something very positive. News like that is horrible because of the fear it casts for the future. We had thoughts like: *She will never talk.She will never walk. She is going to need a wheelchair. What if I am still changing her diaper when she is 25 years old, and I am 50?* All the angst and fear were in the future. All the bad news, difficulty, abnormality, and stress was technically months and years down the line.

If we looked at that day itself, her diagnosis had minimal effect. She laid cutely and quietly in her crib and was a normal newborn. Since that day, there have been many moments of extreme awe and wonder. Kennady looks at us and laughs. She excels beyond our hopes. Then, quickly, those moments are followed by sickness, blank stares, and the hard work of caring for someone unable to care for themselves. We learned early on that this journey was not going to be a quick sprint to the finish line. Instead, we were beginning a series of marathons. We needed to be able to handle the long stretches of tough moments.

One of our heroes, Cindy, has a son with Down syndrome. During this season of our life, Cindy was a source of strength and inspiration. After Kennady's diagnosis, she gave us a statement that completely changed our outlook from that day forward. It was a simple statement, a cliché I had heard for years. However, when we stood in the church hallway that Sunday, she said it, and it was like the heavens opened, beams of light shown down, and angels sang. She calmly said, "Robin, you have to take it day by day." So simple, yet so liberating. I felt peace flood my anguished heart and heavy mind. I didn't have to think about wheelchairs or adult diapers. All I had to do was care for my family *today*. That is it. That is all Kennady needed, and all God expected.

These words originally came from Jesus during his most famous sermon. When he talks about the troubles of life, he says, "So don't worry about **tomorrow**, for tomorrow will bring its own worries. Today's trouble is enough for **today**" (Matthew 6:34, emphasis mine).

A few scriptures before that, he is teaching us how to pray, and he says, "Give us **today** the food we need" (Matthew 6:11, emphasis mine).

He was precise in his wording. He could have said, "Give us the food we need for the next week or month…" However, throughout his message, he emphasizes daily priority. In our modern culture, we are driven to focus on what we don't have today and to channel our energy into obtaining more in the future. Instead, Jesus is saying, look at what you have now and use it to the best of your ability. Indeed, you might not even be around tomorrow. If you are around tomorrow, you can deal with it then.

Many times in scripture, Jesus' schedule is interrupted by individuals needing assistance. He often dropped his plans and healed, scolded, delivered, saved, or related to whoever was there. He had a lot of significant work to do. All the while, the pressure of the cross loomed in the distant horizon. He knew that the cross was inescapable. I am sure he had human thoughts such as: *I wonder if these disciples are actually going to get the job done? The cross is going to take me away from the progress being made.* Jesus was in a strong groove of healing people, teaching profound truth, training the disciples, and modeling the "whole life". He was winning in life by all human measurements.

However, Jesus was well aware of his path toward death. He was to face accusation, persecution, beating and public humility, a "diagnosis" that ended in being nailed physically to a cross, suspended, on display in shame and failure for the world to see. His end was capital punishment in a cruel Roman world.

For a moment, put yourself in Jesus' shoes. How stressful would that be? We struggle with the stress of traffic, bills, and nagging arthritis. Jesus was dealing with being drug to the town square and brutally murdered in front of crying family and friends, embarrassed strangers, and laughing enemies. Most likely, if we faced the impending danger that Jesus did, we would struggle with our daily operations. Studying for tests at school, preparing for work, or finishing projects would be extremely difficult.

Jesus knew that the prospect of future disappointment and imminent danger could cripple our effectiveness today. He knew this not because he is God, but because he experienced it as a human himself! He knew we needed to be effective today, so he preached this powerful truth. Let tomorrow worry about itself. Get it right today. Nail today.

One day, as I was leaving the stage from speaking, a young man stood waiting. "Please help me. I have really messed up, big time," David said with a bowed head. He had served time in prison and was now out on parole. For the last of couple years, he had been living the straight and narrow. However, the night before speaking to me he had broken his curfew and lied to his parole officer about it. I quickly checked my calendar and invited him to come talk with me. The next day, we sat in my office and we walked through the whole situation. David said, "My parole officer has found out the truth and told me that I have to turn myself in. I'm now facing up to ten more months in jail. Honestly, I could run. If I do not get caught and make it until next October, I will be free and clear."

He was wrestling with all the progress he had made. Things had been going so well. He was in love with a young girl, working hard, going to church, and then it fell apart. He wanted to do the right thing and turn himself in but also fought through the idea of simply running. We sat in my office and discussed the broken past and depressing future. He sat with a heavy heart, knowing that he had failed last night. The words of Jesus began ringing in my ears.

When facing the depression of ten more months incarcerated, a few more days of freedom, and no relationship with God, you are going to lose that battle. I told David that day to forget the prison sentence. Forget next week. Forget tomorrow.

I looked at David and shared the lesson that Cindy had shared with me, "David, you need to focus on God for this moment. You need to serve God **today**. We are about to pray, and when we do, we are going to ask God to give you the power to overcome evil today. Then, tomorrow, you are going to wake up again and pray for tomorrow. However, the question you need to figure out is—Am I going to run **tonight**? To answer that question "no," you need to ask God to give you strength for today (your daily bread) and then set up some boundaries for today that will guard you."

Why do we let the prospect of a potentially problematic future cripple our potential for today? What Erica and I have learned is that God gives us exactly what we can handle each day. He incrementally gives us what we can handle. Some days, we think, *Are you sure, God?* It seems extremely difficult, but we pray for God's grace.

Each time He says what He said in scripture: **"My grace is all you need. My power works best in weakness." (2 Corinthians 12:9)**

"No temptation has seized you except what is common to man. And God is faithful; he will not let you be tempted beyond what you can bear. But when you are tempted, he will also provide a way out so that you can stand up under it." (1 Corinthians 10:13)

In David's example, it is easy to see that temptation is

a battle. David was tempted to run and not be accountable for his actions. However, in Erica and my case, there was equal pressure to sin. We were tempted to doubt God. We were tempted to believe that every beautiful dream we had attached to the birth of our daughter was quickly turning into a lifelong nightmare. The devastation of her illness would change our entire lives, and we were tempted to believe that our comfort was more important than God's sovereign plan. Doubting God in this way would cause us stress, depression, fear, anger or resentment. We could quite possibly act out in destructive ways. That is why trusting God on a daily basis is the only way we are able to handle such troubling situations. Trusting God is a pathway to wholeness.

People look at our family and how we handle life and tell us, "We could never do what you do. It's amazing how strong you are." What they do not realize is that God has given us all daily challenges. Each day we grow stronger and stronger. The truth is that Erica and I are very strong. However, that strength is not from us, and it did not happen overnight. It comes from God, and it comes day by day. God gives us a daily allotment of grace to meet the challenges of the day with confidence and peace.

I think it is important to clarify that wholeness is not defined by the absence of difficulty in our lives. When we get focused on the problems and allow fear to captivate our minds and eventually our hearts, then way below the surface of our lives, we begin to believe a lie about who God is. Because we have problems, we fear that God has abandoned us, that God does not care about us, or that we need to perform to earn God's approval. All the while, God is ready to provide the exact amount of grace that we need for that day. The even better news is that God does not measure out enough grace so that we can barely make it. Instead, God provides enough daily grace to make us feel as though the challenges in our lives will not overcome us; they will not define us. We feel thorough, inner peace.

All parts of God's creation grow at their own pace, yet each day is vital to their health and growth. How we steward each day determines where we end up in the future. Just as walls are built one brick at a time, we link together days with God until we look back and realize He has created in us a wall of strength. As you face the day, I invite you to look for the graces that abound in it for you. The kind and loving providence of God that is present in your day is waiting to be noticed. Let the future remain where it belongs, in the tomorrows. This is how I have made it eighteen years. This is how wholeness works.

CHAPTER FIFTEEN

LIVING BY FAITH

Faith is like radar that sees through the fog—the reality of things at a distance that the human eye cannot see.

—Corrie Ten Boom

When Erica and I planted the church that we pastor in San Marcos, Texas, we were rookies. I was 26 years old and very green. I was so nervous that people would ask me questions about what happened to the dinosaurs or how the book of Revelation was going to play out. I am happy to report that I have not been asked those questions yet! God has been so faithful to us along the way and helped with every need. One of the ways God helped us was by sending us some people to support, pray, work, and give alongside us. We started with about thirty people, each of them uniquely invested in this congregation. We worked so hard. When people ask how we grew to a membership of over 2,000 people, I quickly point to the sacrifice and seeds sown by these thirty people (and all those who followed).

Jane Murry could be my favorite. Please do not tell the rest of PromiseLand church about this! Actually, all of you members that are reading this book, if you knew Jane, you would say the same thing! Jane is her actual name. I am not going to change it to protect her. Everyone needs to know her, and everyone needs to learn from her. Jane was 50 years old when we started the church and had suffered from cystic fibrosis her whole life.

According to the Cystic Fibrosis Foundation, cystic fibrosis is a progressive, genetic disease that causes persistent lung infections and limits the ability to breathe over time. In people with CF, a defective gene causes a thick, sticky buildup of mucus in the lungs, pancreas, and other organs. In the lungs, the mucus clogs the airways and traps bacteria leading to infections, extensive lung damage, and eventually, respiratory failure. In the pancreas, the mucus prevents the release of digestive enzymes that allow the body to break down food and absorb vital nutrients.

Because of this condition, Jane lived with some level of pneumonia all the time. She was unable to eat certain foods and struggled to maintain a healthy weight. Every year, her pneumonia hospitalized her for weeks. Every day, for decades, Jane would do multiple breathing treatments. Jane was married to a wonderful husband, Ernie. They defeated the odds and gave birth to a brilliant son, "Little Ernie." For years, Jane raised her son and helped her husband with their small business. In 2003, when PromiseLand came to town, Jane decided to take the leap with us and be a part of our church plant. She worked as hard as she could with us. Jane would greet people at the door, make phone calls, write notes of encouragement, attend services, participate in the message, and more.

Typically, when I go to the hospital or someone's house to pray for them, I find them in a very dark place physically and spiritually. They need encouragement and strength from a pastor. I would often visit Jane's house to pray for her, and when I went into the room, I am the one that received something from Jane. She would slowly pull off the oxygen mask and start talking about how good God was to her. She would start listing all of the blessings in her life. I would sit there weeping and think, *How could this be happening?*

For years, I knew the day would come for Jane's funeral. In fact, on one of our visits, Jane handed me a manila folder and simply said, "All the details are in there for my funeral." I took the folder and did not want to think about it. Jane had meant so much to us. How could we continue without her bold faith and subtle leadership? However, the reality was that Jane had already beaten the odds and defied all the doctors' prognoses. Kids born in the 1950s with cystic fibrosis did not live to be over 50 years old. On July of 2013, her pneumonia grew to an intense level, and Jane peacefully passed on to eternity. I was both sad for her loss and grateful for her presence in my life. I prayed fervently for God to give me some Word from scripture to honor Jane's life and paint the picture of her faithful walk.

I opened up the book of Hebrews and started to read about the heroes of faith in chapter 11. If you have never read this passage, I highly recommend that you explore it often. It starts with a description of faith: "Faith shows the reality of what we hope for; it is the evidence of things we cannot see." (Hebrews 11:1)

The writer systematically recounts the heroes of faith in the Old and New Testaments. Each is listed by name, with a couple of sentences about their remarkable life and faith-filled journey with God. It is so encouraging and uplifting to see men and women listed here. I have heard this passage preached dozens of times and am so thankful for it. However, as I read through it this time, I realized that this passage did not relate to Jane because, though Jane had lived a life of incredible faith, she had not seen the apparent rewards in this life. In fact, Jane had been cheated quite a bit in this life for all the beautiful seeds she had sown.

I could not use this passage or relate it to Jane until I kept reading and discovered a jewel at the end of the chapter.

But others were tortured, refusing to turn from God in order to be set free. They placed their hope in a better life after the resurrection. Some were jeered at, and their backs were cut open with whips. Others were chained in prisons. Some died by stoning, some were sawed in half, and others were killed with the sword. Some went about wearing skins of sheep and goats, destitute and oppressed and mistreated. They were too good for this world, wandering over deserts and mountains, hiding in caves and holes in the ground. All these people earned a good reputation because of their faith, yet none of them received all that God had promised. For God had something better in mind for us, so that they would not reach perfection without us. (Hebrews 11:35–40)

I found Jane in the section of verses 35–40, among the heroes that will never be fully recognized for their contributions on this side of life. These were the people that kept living the life of faith and walking the journey with Jesus. As verse 38 says, "They were too good for this world, wandering over deserts and mountains, hiding in caves and holes in the ground."

Some of you reading this book will see tremendous blessing this year. You will find favor and all the recognition for which you have worked. God places you in the first part of Hebrews chapter 11. Then, there will be others of us that walk the final parts of Hebrews chapter 11. We will not see the immediate fruit of our labors. The incredible thing about God's Kingdom is that being whole today is not predicated on either one. Being whole in Christ is completely detached from the outer or surface parts of our lives.

In sixteen years of pastoring this church, I have never seen anyone embody the message of this book like Jane. Jane's life exemplified a person trusting in something beyond herself, beyond medicine, beyond therapy. Jane Murry was a whole person. God had made her whole. Her physical body was very broken, but way down deep, her soul and spirit were healthier than anyone else I knew. There was a peace that flowed below the surface and worked its way public. That peace was rooted in a belief that God could be trusted.

Jane had faith that she was forgiven and completely accepted as God's daughter. Jane understood that she and the doctors had lost control many years ago, but that did not matter because God still had every detail in the palm of His hand. Jane rested in this reality so steadfastly that no matter what challenge came her way, she was going to be ok. Jane's smile lit up a room. Her laugh was contagious. Jane was so resolute and confident in her position with God that it transcended the facts of her life. Her life could be painful, and the future was very much uncertain, but peace guarded her heart and mind.

Whether we see victories in this part of life or we face persecution, we are tempted to believe something that is not true about God. We are tempted to live without faith and to try to live life on our own. When things are going well, and we are hitting all of our goals, we are tempted to take credit and think that God is there simply to help us along the way. When we are failing to reach our quotas, and we experience pain or heaviness, we are tempted to believe that God does not care, is disengaged, or is unable to help with our details. None of those lies are true. Both of those scenarios lead us to a broken existence. Someone on either of those trails will eventually find themselves far from home. They will search and search, thinking that changing something about their life will lead them back to peace.

Jesus Christ understood this dilemma and lived out the solution for us. He is the ultimate example of how to face victory and trouble. Jesus Christ is the solution for the most disturbing uncertainties about ourselves and God. Only Jesus can bring healing to our hearts, give us the intimacy of family, and promise the hope of our resurrection and eternal life. **We are accepted as His kids, and God is in complete control of all that seems to be chaos.** We will be rewarded. There will be a day when all the tears are dried, and peace will reign in a new heaven and a new earth. Jesus' resurrection tells us that death is defeated, not just for Jesus, but for all of us. We will be resurrected and live with God forever in a new heaven and a new earth. In that place, we will be known as we were known here in this world, but sin's effects will no longer be a reality. All the broken and dark things that have happened will not just be forgotten; they will be undone.

Until that day of ultimate freedom and redemption comes, let's live like this: Let us strip off every weight that slows us down, especially the sin that so easily trips us up. And let us run with endurance the race God has set before us. We do this by keeping our eyes on Jesus, the champion who initiates and perfects our faith. Because of the joy awaiting him, he endured the cross, disregarding its shame. Now he is seated in the place of honor beside God's throne. Think of all the hostility he endured from sinful people; then you won't become weary and give up. (Hebrews 12:1–3)

EPILOGUE

Kennady is now 18 years old and finishing up her final year at Hays High School! We are so thankful for each day that we are able to hang out with her. She continues to light up a room and make a difference for those who take the time to hang out with her.

We live near San Marcos, TX, which borders the hill country between Austin and San Antonio. A couple of years ago, we purchased our own little chunk of land and built a house in a very rural pocket of our area. We are literally at the end of the road and nestled high above the gorgeous Blanco River.

Our sons are classic teenagers. Both are an active part of our local schools' football teams, church youth group, and, of course, spend quite a bit of time in the game room diving into the world of Fortnite!

Erica has built a thriving midwifery practice. In fact, as I type this epilogue she is at the birth of a precious new baby. I'm biased, but I will say she is absolutely an incredible midwife who not only births babies, but loves and serves the community. She is honored to play a part in these momentous occasions.

I continue to serve as senior pastor at PromiseLand Church with multiple campuses in San Marcos and Lockhart, TX. I also work with our affiliate churches in Austin, Marble Falls, Drippings Springs, and Waco. What a privilege to play a part in God's work in this area. There are so many people in our church family who play an active role in our lives.

When we zoom out of the details and see the entire landscape of our life, it is breathtaking. It is impossible. *How could this happen?* I would have never dreamed that this type of life was possible with a daughter who was unable to do anything. My only thoughts went toward compromise. I thought I would have to give up so much to live with such disability. Everything points back to the power of God and the incredible grace that transcends our circumstances.

Of course, this is exciting when we think about the future. What lies ahead? What lies ahead if God is able to do anything He wants regardless of our limitations? We have not seen it. We have not heard it. In fact, our minds cannot really comprehend how much He has prepared for us.

SOURCES

Holy Bible: New Living Translation. Wheaton, Ill: Tyndale House Publishers, 2004.

Scazzero, Pete. *Emotionally Healthy Spirituality.* Zondervan Books. 2006.

Ellenberger, Henri F. *The Discovery of the Unconscious.* 1970. p. 147 and p. 406.

Holy Bible: King James Version. Thomas Nelson. 1991

Shakespeare, William. *The Tragedy of Hamlet, Prince of Denmark.* New Folger's ed. New York: Washington Square Press/Pocket Books, 1992.

"rest", Merriam-Webster.com. Merriam Webster, 2019. Web October 11, 2019.

Study Bible: English Standard Version. Wheaton, Ill: Crossway Bibles, 2007.

Hendriksen, W., & Kistemaker, S. J. *Exposition of the Gospel According to Luke.* Grand Rapids: Baker Book House 1953-2001. Vol. 11, p. 756.

Holy Bible: New English Translation. Biblical Studies Press, L.L.C.. 2005

Keller, Timothy. *Prayer, Experiencing the Awe and Intimacy of God*. Penguin Books. 2016.

Peterson, Eugene. *Working the Angles: The Shape of Pastoral Integrity*. Wm. B. Eerdmans Publishing Co. Grand Rapids, MI. 1987. p. 49.

Nicholas, Johanna Grant, and Ann E Geers. *Effects of Early Auditory Experience on the Spoken Language of Deaf Children at 3 Years of Age*. Ear and Hearing, U.S. National Library of Medicine, June 2006, www.ncbi.nlm.nih.gov/pmc/articles/PMC2880472/.

Siegenthaler, Andrew. *The Power of the Seed*. February 4, 2007. www.christcovenantcullman.org/sermonnotes/notes-02-04-07.html.

Millard, Bart; Kipley, Pete. Word of God Speak. Inot Records, 2002.

King, Martin Luther. "Letter from Birmingham Jail." 16 Apr. 1963. Web. November 22, 2019.

Boom, Corrie Ten. *Corrie Ten Boom Quotes*. 2019. christian-quotes.ochristian.com/Corrie-Ten-Boom-Quotes/.

About Cystic Fibrosis. CF Foundation, 2019, www.cff.org/What-is-CF/About-Cystic-Fibrosis/.

ABOUT THE AUTHOR

Robin Steele is the founder and lead pastor of PromiseLand Church in San Marcos, TX. Over the last sixteen years, they have gone from thirty people to a membership well over 2,000. PromiseLand is a multi-ethnic, multi-generational congregation that impacts people from all walks of life. Robin loves to teach, disciple, invest in pastors, hunt, fish, snow ski and ride his mountain bike (real fast) over crazy terrain!

In 2001, Robin and his wife, Erica, received the news that their newborn baby had a severe brain abnormality and would only live for six months or so. Their daughter, Kennady, just turned 18 years old and continues to defeat the odds. She lives with many disabilities and requires twenty-four hour care. Robin speaks all over the world about the incredible life lessons they have learned along the way. They have two sons as well: Jude, and Avery.

Follow their journey at:

mademeaningful.com

Facebook.com/mademeaningful

Instagram.com/mademeaningful

Twitter.com/RobinSteele